GLUTEN-FREE PASTA

GLUTEN-FREE
PASTA

More than 100 Fast and Flavorful Recipes

with Low- and No-Carb Options

By Robin Asbell

PHOTOGRAPHY BY
Jason Varney

Running Press
PHILADELPHIA · LONDON

Published by Running Press,
A Member of the Perseus Books Group

Books published by Running Press are available at special discounts for bulk purchases in the United States by corporations, institutions, and other organizations. For more information, please contact the Special Markets Department at the Perseus Books Group, 2300 Chestnut Street, Suite 200, Philadelphia, PA 19103, or call (800) 810-4145, ext. 5000, or e-mail special.markets@perseusbooks.com.

ISBN 978-0-7624-4967-5

Library of Congress Control Number: 2013943525

E-book ISBN 978-0-7624-5178-4

9 8 7 6 5 4 3 2 1
Digit on the right indicates the number of this printing

Cover and interior design by Joshua McDonnell
Edited by Kristen Green Wiewora
Typography: Avenir and Kabel
Food styling by Carrie Purcell
Prop styling by Paige Hicks

Running Press Book Publishers
2300 Chestnut Street
Philadelphia, PA 19103-4371

Visit us on the web!
www.offthemenublog.com

Dedication

I dedicate this book to my mother, Marilyn Calhoun, whose food allergies had the unexpected benefit of motivating me to investigate cooking for special diets many years ago. Of course, the support of my family and my sweetheart, Stanley, carries me through all my projects and endeavors, and I thank them.

Acknowledgments

No author is an island, and I count my agent, Jennifer Griffin, as a supporting player in shaping this project and cheering me on every step of the way.

My fabulous friends Carol Fenster, Jill O'Connor, and Fran Costigan provided tech support and moral support, and I thank them for their generosity.

My intrepid recipe testers—Kristine Vick, Lisa Genis, Melodie Bahan, and Elizabeth Sellett—helped me immensely, too, making sure everything worked as well in their kitchens as it did in mine.

The good folks at Running Press took my work and transformed it with beautiful photographs, engaging layouts, and a national campaign, and I thank Kristen Green Wiewora, designer Joshua McDonnell, photographer Jason Varney, and others.

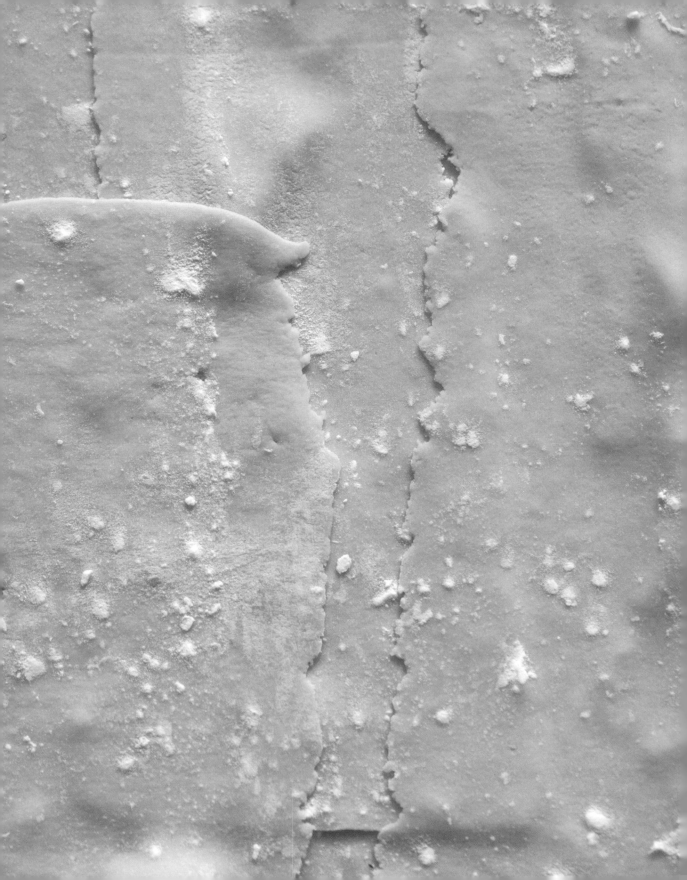

Reimagining Pasta

Pasta. Noodles. They are comfort on a plate. In infinite variations, pasta and noodles feed the world and cross all cultural divides. If you are broke, you can fill up with instant ramen at four packs for a dollar. If you are flush, you can pay top dollar for a plate of handmade artisanal pasta gilded with truffles and lobster. Hole-in-the-wall noodle stands, authentic soba shops, and Italian pasta palaces inspire cult-like devotion. Rich or poor, people the world over crave the soft, slippery noodle and the toothsome bite of a good pasta.

Pasta is so beloved that it is one of the most grieved foods that a gluten-free (GF) diet takes off the plate. Pasta and noodles have a big place on our menus and in our hearts, so it is tough realizing that Grandma's lasagna will never be okay for us again. The deep emotional pull that we have toward our comfort foods is tough to resist. It's this passion for pasta that fuels us in the search for great alternatives, and I've been on the case for some time now. You can stop grieving. You will eat pasta again.

The old debate over who invented the noodle is a good illustration of the ubiquity of the food. Did the Chinese invent the noodle, only to have Marco Polo take the idea to the Italians? It turns out that ancient remnants found in China show that a noodle was made there 4,000 years ago. That earliest noodle was made with millet flour, from the staple grain of the day, which by the way, is gluten-free. Historians tell us that ancient Romans made their first lasagna with wheat-based noodles that were baked before layering in the pan, as early as the first century, long before Marco Polo's journey. The Arabs are credited with inventing dried pasta and revolutionizing portable foods, which they spread to Italy.

So you see, pasta and noodles had to be invented, tweaked, and perfected over a couple of thousand years. And now, because you can't eat gluten anymore, it's time to reinvent them again. The world of gluten-free pastas has gotten so much better so quickly, and you may not have tried the latest, best one. Your local Asian market is a treasure trove of gluten-free noodles, and there is no rule that says you can only use them in pad thai or pho. Pasta and noodles have always been easy to prepare, and they can still be your fast, flavorful, fallback foods for busy nights.

Fresh, handmade pasta may seem like just a dream now that you are gluten-free, but it doesn't have to be. With my recipes, you can make your own pastas and roll them out to make thick, homey noodles or thin, sophisticated sheets for lasagna, ravioli, and all your Italian favorites. Missing the dumplings you used to get at dim sum? You can make those too, and they are really good without gluten.

Conceptual Noodles

It's time to push the concept of pasta to include not just brown rice spaghetti, but also silky zucchini strand spaghetti and curly sweet potato noodles. With an open mind, you might find that the spicy sesame noodles you loved as takeout can actually be replaced by slivers of leafy greens, tenderized by the tangy sauce that was the main event all along. If you take a playful approach, just about anything cut in long strips can stand in for spaghetti.

If you are avoiding carbs, you can make my low-carb Egg Crêpe "Noodles" (page 38), or even use shirataki noodles in these recipes. The vegetable noodle options are also a great way to go low carb. If you want to follow a Paleo diet, these recipes can work for you.

In fact, most of these dishes have a different balance between pasta, sauce, and vegetables than you may be used to. It's my philosophy that vegetables should take up more room on the plate, so I pump up the plant presence in relation to the pasta. You can still get your pasta cravings met, but with more veggies and fewer carbs.

It's time to explore the concept of what pasta is and what it can be. You found this book because you are gluten-free, but consider yourself lucky. You are going to take a journey with pasta and noodles, and you will never look at them the same way again.

Reasons for Going Gluten-Free

Going gluten-free is all the rage these days. If you have been avoiding gluten for over five or ten years, then you have seen a sea change in the availability of gluten-free products due to the growing numbers of customers who want to buy them. Back in the eighties and early nineties, when I first started baking wheat-free items for my customers, all I could get was gritty brown rice flour, some starches, and one brand of frozen bread that resembled a sponge. Now, even a small grocery store might well have a few gluten-free cookies, crackers, breads, and pastas tucked in next to the soymilk.

How has this happened? The growth in numbers of gluten-avoiding people has come from several sources, and it will probably continue to rise. There are lots of theories and speculation about this growth, and it will probably be a long time before it's all settled. So, let's look at the main reasons for getting off the gluten.

1. Celiac sprue is a genetically inherited autoimmune response to gluten, and it can be life threatening. When a person with celiac sprue eats gluten, her immune system attacks her own tissues and damages the villi in the intestines. These damaged villi cannot digest food properly or absorb nutrients, and they also become porous, releasing the offending substance into the bloodstream. While many celiac sprue sufferers present digestive symptoms, many do not. The toxic

combination of the inability to absorb essential nutrients and the inflammation caused by a porous gut leads to a myriad of problems, ranging from skin and joint issues to infertility, osteoporosis, anemia, and depression.

In a frustrating turn, doctors don't diagnose celiac sprue very well. According to the University of Chicago Celiac Disease Center, 97 percent of celiacs are still undiagnosed. The center estimates that three million Americans are living with the disease. It also says that the number of people with celiac sprue seems to double every fifteen to twenty years, but the reasons for that are still debatable.

If a person has celiac sprue, she can only heal and thrive by eliminating gluten from her diet. Growing awareness has helped, and it has increased the number of people who seek diagnosis.

2. Wheat allergies are also an immune response to wheat and gluten. Wheat is one of the top eight allergenic foods. Symptoms of wheat allergies might include skin problems, histamine responses (such as a runny nose, a swollen tongue, or sneezing), abdominal distress, or even anaphylaxis. An allergist can run a relatively simple skin-prick test and determine whether you are allergic to wheat. Some people who are allergic to wheat can tolerate other members of the wheat family, like spelt or kamut, while some cannot. Allergies can develop at any time in life, and they can also go away, if the sufferer avoids the allergen for a long period of time.

3. Gluten intolerance and gluten sensitivity are broad terms for conditions that are not fully understood or easily diagnosed. Basically, you may find that you have symptoms that only go away when you stop eating gluten. Doctors are often very skeptical of these self-diagnoses, so you may have a hard time convincing your practitioner that you have a problem. It's becoming common for people with stubborn health issues to try an elimination diet after standard medical intervention has been unsuccessful. This is basically a tool for figuring out which foods agree with you. A doctor can assist you in this, or you can do it yourself. If you eliminate all gluten from your diet for six weeks, you will give your body time to let you know if it is happier without it.

4. Growing numbers of parents of autistic and ADHD children are removing gluten from their children's diets and reporting that their behavior is improved. Athletes are trying out gluten-free diets and insisting that it helps performance. People are giving up gluten and reporting clearer thinking, weight loss, and improved health. As of now, experts can't agree on whether these people are just feeling better because they have made their diets cleaner and healthier, or whether there is something else to it. A growing group of people believe that changes in the genetic makeup of wheat over the years have made it into a food that our bodies can't tolerate. It is true that plant breeders have worked to create strains of wheat with higher gluten contents and more complex genes.

While science catches up with all of this, you may well decide that living without gluten helps you. If a food doesn't agree with you, it only makes sense to stop eating it. We all have individualized systems, and finding your optimum diet takes some experimentation. The only caveat that a dietitian would add is that if you take a food out of your diet, make sure that you replace the nutrients that it provided.

So Now What?

Restaurant outings, family gatherings, and work lunches will be different now that you are avoiding one of the most common foods that we eat. It doesn't help that you probably really like those foods, too. Create safe zones for yourself, and as you go along, you will expand them. Search online and find a few restaurants that have gluten-free options. When you're there, make sure to ask. Talk to the manager if the server seems unsure. A typical Chinese or Thai meal based on rice noodles might look safe, but it may be made with soy sauce that contains wheat. Many Chinese dishes are made from prepared sauces that could contain wheat starch or flour. The same water might be used to cook the noodles made from wheat, too. That's why you need to seek out places that have protocols in place for keeping your foods free of gluten.

Your friends and family may need a little help at first, too. To be safe, you should bring your own food while everybody catches up with your new diet. A package of brown rice spaghetti or a casserole from the Baked Pastas chapter may well be your best accessory when heading out to a gathering at someone's home.

At the grocery store, you will need to learn some new habits. Be very careful about label reading, since gluten and wheat lurk in places you would not expect. Wheat, barley, rye, triticale, spelt, and kamut all contain gluten, so watch for those words. As mentioned, some people who are allergic to wheat can tolerate spelt and kamut, which are ancient forms of wheat, but celiacs and other gluten-intolerant people must avoid them. Seitan, also called mock duck, is pure gluten. Most soy sauces are made with wheat, and miso might contain barley. Couscous, bulghur, and most pastas are wheat based.

Packaged foods with long ingredient lists are often a source of mysteriously named ingredients that you must avoid. Hydrolyzed vegetable protein, modified food starch, malt or malt flavor, dextrin, and maltodextrin may be made from wheat. Any vaguely named ingredient, like "seasonings" or "flavorings" may well be, too. To be safe, look for the contact information on the package and contact the manufacturer.

What Gluten Does and How We Work Around It

If you are wondering why gluten and wheat are included in so many foods, it's because gluten is used to create structure. Gluten is a composite created when two proteins, glutenin and gliadin, are mixed with water and form hydrogen bonds, allowing them to form a sturdy network. It's this unique ability that has made gluten-containing grains and flours the choice for making bread and pasta. Doughs made with gluten are springy and stretchy, and the gluten makes the finished bread hold an open crumb or a pasta hold together in boiling water and have a chewy texture.

When it comes to pasta, eliminating gluten has been a challenge, but one that is being met with more success every day. If you tried GF pasta ten years ago and gave up on it, it's time to try it again. GF pastas have improved rapidly, while traditional Asian rice and buckwheat noodles have always been good. Of course, without that gluten structure, some features are different. GF pastas are delicate, and the window of time in which they are perfectly cooked is much shorter than the cooking window of wheat pasta. All you can do is set the timer sooner than it says on the package, and start testing—and test often. Once your pasta is al dente, serve it forth. You will also find that GF pastas are very absorbent, soaking up their sauces and soup broths much more than wheat pastas do. Because of this, it is best to add the pasta to the soup just before serving. Leftovers may be different the next day, but they will still be good. Most of these recipes have relatively dry sauces, so the pastas don't have a ton of liquid to drink in.

The good news is that there are other ways to accomplish the tasks that gluten performs in your food, without making you sick! As you will see—for example, in the fresh pasta and dumpling wrapper recipes in this book—I will be employing some ingredients that may be new to you. **Here is a quick introduction.** ⟶

Your Gluten-Free Pantry

Flours

White rice flour: This flour is used to thicken sauces and is made from regular white rice.

Sweet rice flour: Made from "sweet," or "glutinous," rice, this flour is a little stickier than regular white rice flour, and despite the name, it contains no gluten at all.

Sorghum flour: Sorghum grain is grown in the United States, and it has all the nutrients of whole grain, with a mild flavor.

Millet flour: Millet has a pretty yellow color, which makes the pasta look nice and eggy instead of pale. It's also a whole grain, with 15 percent protein, high fiber, and B vitamins and minerals. Using some whole grains to make your pasta adds nutrition and makes it a healthier food.

Tapioca starch: Tapioca is made from the root of the cassava plant, which is native to Brazil and grown in tropical countries. It's a neutral and very absorbent starch.

Arrowroot starch: A starch made from the root of the arrowroot plant, native to South America, arrowroot is similar to both tapioca and cornstarch.

Whey protein powder: This is sold as an ingredient to use in smoothies and protein shakes, often in the supplements section. Make sure you get plain, not vanilla or chocolate. You can use any left over for adding protein to baked goods and smoothies.

Binders

Xanthan gum: Made from corn that is fermented by a microorganism called *Xanthomonas campestris*, xanthan gum is a fine powder that forms a paste when mixed with water. When baked or boiled, the gum becomes firm, giving gluten-free foods a sturdy texture. Anecdotally, I have found that some people may have a difficult time digesting xanthan gum, so I only use a small amount in the pasta.

Guar gum: Guar gum is made from the seed of a plant grown in India and Pakistan. It contains a concentrated fiber and is used in many commercially prepared foods as a thickener. It works the same way that xanthan gum does in replacing gluten, but it seems a little softer in the final product. Oddly enough, it is used in many industrial applications, including hydraulic fracturing, or "fracking," where it is mixed with water to inject in the ground and extract oil.

Eggs: The most familiar gluten-free binder, eggs make delicious and supple pasta. They also add protein, an important component of a good GF blend.

Condiments: Gluten-free versions of Asian sauces are getting easier and easier to find. Wok Mei, Panda, and Choy Sum are some brands to seek out. Wheat-free tamari is made by Eden brand and several others.

An Incomplete Guide to Gluten-Free Pastas and Noodles

Wherever you live, there should be a few gluten-free pastas showing up on your grocer's shelves. If not, request them. Because each region, city, and individual store carries a different lineup of gluten-free flours and pastas, you may find yourself visiting more than one store to find good selections. The good news is that dry pasta keeps for months, so stocking up when you find the shape or brand you are seeking is a great idea. I've tried every brand available, and here is my take. I must tell you that I lean toward whole grains whenever possible, for nutritional reasons. Luckily, many of the best pastas are whole grain.

My personal favorite is Tinkyada, and I think many people agree, since it seems to be the most common on grocers' shelves. I've also tried Pappardelle's trumpets, which are a splurge, and found them to be outstanding. That being said, the rest of the pastas that I tried are also very good. If you

can see the pasta through the package and it is pale white, it is probably a little more delicate and has a more neutral taste. Corn-based pastas have an appealing golden color and an agreeable sweetness.

Where I live, I can buy RP's fresh pasta from the cold case at several stores. It is an excellent product, and it comes in several shapes as well as stuffed. It is available online, too. Pasta Loioco is another brand available online, as are a large selection of dried GF pastas and noodles. Artisans in your area may well be introducing gluten-free fresh pastas for sale, so seek them out.

The gluten-free market is growing and changing so quickly, I fully expect that new brands and styles of GF pasta will appear on store shelves before this book arrives in bookstores, so keep an eye out for new and exciting developments. **The following list serves to illustrate just how many options there are out there.**

White and Brown Rice Pastas

Bionaturae (rice, potato, and soy)

OrgraN (brown rice, rice and corn, buckwheat)

Jovial (brown rice)

Tinkyada (brown rice)

Schar (corn, white rice, and multigrain)

Annie Chun's (white and brown rice)

Hodgson Mill (brown rice)

Heartland (white rice)

Farmo (corn and white rice)

Goldbaum's Kosher (brown rice)

Pastariso (brown rice)

Lundberg couscous (brown rice)

Corn Pastas

Mrs. Leeper's (corn)

DeBoles (white rice, corn, and quinoa and amaranth blends)

Pasta d'Oro (corn)

Sam Mills (corn)

Schar (corn)

Le Veneziane (corn)

Riso Bello (rice, corn, buckwheat)

Farmo (corn)

Heartland (corn)

BiAglut (corn, potato, and lupin)

Barkat (corn)

Seitenbacher (corn and lupin)

Buckwheat and Quinoa Pastas

Ancient Harvest (quinoa)

OrgraN (quinoa, multigrain)

Riso Bello (rice, corn, and buckwheat)

Eden Soba (100% buckwheat only)

King Soba (variety of buckwheat and other GF noodles)

Refrigerated and Frozen Fresh Pastas

Pappardelle's Della Terra (brown rice, tapioca, corn, and quinoa)

Contes (frozen ravioli, gnocchi, and other pastas)

Vegetable Noodles

Miracle Noodle (shirataki)

Gold Mine (kelp)

Multiple Sensitivities and Special Diets

In my years of teaching gluten-free cooking classes and private-cheffing, I have met many people who are not just dealing with gluten issues but also have other allergies and sensitivities. Some of the top allergenic foods include dairy, eggs, soy, corn, shellfish, fish, peanuts, and tree nuts. There are also growing numbers of people practicing diets like the Paleo diet, who avoid grains, dairy, soy, and beans. In cooking for people with long lists of foods to avoid, I have come up with ways to work around most issues. That is why you have the option to use so many different "pastas" here. People who are eating low carb or grain free can use egg crêpes, veggie strand noodles, or shirataki noodles.

Dairy: Use unsweetened or plain non-dairy milk in place of cow's milk in recipes. For cream or half-and-half that will be boiled, use well-shaken canned coconut milk. For butter, substitute coconut oil, margarine, or olive oil.

Eggs: The Basic Fresh Pasta recipe (page 29) in this book contains eggs. I made countless eggless versions, but none of them were superior to dried pasta, so I recommend that you just opt for dried. In other recipes that call for eggs, such as for the lasagna filling, you can just leave the eggs out and it will be a little less solid, or blend in a couple of tablespoons of arrowroot starch per pound of ricotta. In stir-fried noodle dishes like Pad Thai (page 145), mix a tablespoon of arrowroot with a couple of tablespoons of water and add that instead of eggs.

Soy: There are some tofu dishes in this book, and you can always substitute chicken breast. To avoid tamari, there is now a product called "coconut aminos" that replicates soy sauce but contains no soy. Fish sauce can also stand in for soy sauce.

Corn: In most of these recipes, you will use arrowroot or tapioca instead of cornstarch, and there are just a few recipes that use corn. Just substitute another vegetable for the corn.

Shellfish: If you can have fish, then firm-textured white fish can replace shrimp in most recipes. Just cut it in inch-wide cubes, and it should cook in about the same amount of time. You can also use chicken or tofu.

Fish: Chicken or firm tofu can stand in for fish.

Peanuts and tree nuts: Find a nut that you can eat and use it instead. Almond butter and sunflower butter are popular substitutes for peanut butter. If a recipe calls for a sprinkling of peanuts at the end, you can either use another nut or seed or simply use something crunchy, such as diced water chestnuts.

Pasta Equivalents: Using All Your Options

While you are exploring the wide world of gluten-free pasta alternatives, it will help you immensely to have a starting point. Using this list, you can substitute one noodle for another noodle, all by volume. So a recipe calling for 8 ounces of spaghetti, for example, can be made with an alternative that makes 4 cups of finished strands.

Asian Noodles

Shirataki and konjac: 8 ounces make 1¼ cups cooked noodles

Soba: 8 ounces make 4 cups cooked noodles

Cellophane noodles (bean threads): 8 ounces make 5 cups cooked noodles

Rice: 8 ounces vermicelli or wide flat noodles make 4 cups cooked noodles

Explore Asian soybean spaghetti: 8 ounces make 4 cups cooked noodles

Handmade Pastas

One recipe of Egg Crêpe "Noodles" makes 6 cups cooked noodles

One recipe of Basic Fresh Pasta makes 4 cups of cooked pasta or 8 pasta sheets, 5 inches wide and 17 inches long

Dried Pastas

1 pound dried spaghetti makes 8 cups cooked noodles

1 pound dried penne makes 8 cups cooked noodles

1 pound dried macaroni makes 8 cups cooked noodles

1 pound dried small shells makes 6 cups cooked noodles

1 pound dried fusilli makes 7 cups cooked noodles

1 pound dried pagodas makes 8 cups cooked noodles

1 (10-ounce) box brown rice couscous makes about 5 cups cooked couscous

Serving Sizes

These dishes can be served as main courses or as sides. Serving sizes are often subjective. A hungry adult might plow through a recipe that could serve four without a problem. If you are eating a big plate of pasta for dinner with no sides, you will need more than if you are having noodles as a component in a multicourse meal, with a filling salad and a main course. With that in mind, I gave all the recipes a ranging yield, such as two to four or four to six servings.

In conventional cookery, two ounces of dry pasta is a recommended serving size. If you are doing a pasta and sauce pairing, go with this measurement as a start, or with the equivalent of two cups of cooked pasta. The serving recommendations in these recipes are based on the final volume of the dish, rather than a serving size of pasta.

Nutrition

1 ounce dried 100% buckwheat soba noodles (¼ cup cooked): 100 calories, 22 g carb, 3 g protein (4.5 mg omega 3, 57.1 mg omega 6, 2% of daily potassium, 10% of daily phosphorus, 2.5% of daily zinc)

1 ounce dried Tinkyada brown rice spaghetti (½ cup cooked): 100 calories, 22 g carb, 2 g protein (4% of daily iron)

1 ounce dried Schar spaghetti (½ cup cooked): 100 calories, 21 g carb, 2.5 g protein

1 ounce drained shirataki noodles (½ cup cooked): 5 calories, 0.6 g carb, 0.25 g protein

1 ounce drained konjac (glucomannan) noodles (½ cup cooked): 0 calories, 0 carb, 0 protein (very high soluble fiber)

1 ounce dried rice noodles (½ cup cooked): 102 calories, 23 g carb, 1 g protein

1 ounce mung bean threads: (heaping ½ cup cooked) 98 calories, 24 g carb (calcium and iron)

FRESH
PASTAS

You can certainly make most of the recipes in this book without ever making fresh pasta. Using a dried alternative is quick and convenient. But I hope that you will give fresh pasta a try. We have all had the experience of eating a prepared food like mayonnaise, or drinking orange juice from concentrate every morning, and thinking it is just fine. Then one day, you get a taste of homemade mayonnaise or just-squeezed juice. You suddenly realize that the fresh version is completely different and superior.

If you have been led to believe that pasta takes all day to make or requires great skill, you will be pleasantly surprised. Simply measure the ingredients, put them in the stand mixer, and beat for two minutes, or mix in the food processor. You have the option of rolling the dough out by hand or in a pasta-rolling machine, or you can use a pasta press or extruder (I used the Kitchen Aid attachment). Either way, once you get some practice, you will find that the rolling goes quickly. Once your pasta dough has been formed into sheets, you can use it for fresh lasagna or cannelloni, or slice it into noodles of varying widths.

If you do not already have an accurate kitchen scale, let me urge you to get one now. You will absolutely have more accuracy and better results in making fresh pasta if you weigh your flours. It's so much more accurate—and easy—to simply spoon flour into a cup sitting on a scale. No sifting, no tapping the cup, no leveling: just weigh it and know that you are getting the right amount. The gluten-free flours that you will be using all have very different weights per cup, so it just works better to go by weight.

Once you have made your pasta dough, use your scale to divide the dough into portions. Four-ounce pieces fit in the pasta roller easily and are a convenient amount of pasta to use in recipes. Simply divide a single one-pound batch of pasta dough into four pieces, then weigh each and add or subtract a little dough as necessary to make the portions even. Then form each portion into a rectangular shape. This is a crucial step if you want evenly shaped sheets of pasta. Once you have your portions cut and shaped, put them in a resealable plastic bag and refrigerate for up to two days, or cover them with plastic wrap on the counter as you work, so they don't dry out.

Another secret to success is to use plenty of starch while rolling out the dough. If rolling by hand, clear your counter and dust it liberally with tapioca or arrowroot starch, place your dough on the starch, and then start shaping and rolling.

For hand-rolled noodles or spaghetti, form a rectangle and roll it out as you would for lasagna sheets. Spread plenty of starch on the counter, and periodically slide a spatula or bench knife under the sheet and move it to make sure it is not sticking. It's okay if it doesn't come out perfectly shaped since you are cutting it up anyway. Then, either slice it with a pizza cutter if you have one, or loosely roll the sheet into a flat cylinder and cut across the roll with a knife to make noodles. Fluff and toss with starch, and store in a covered tub in the refrigerator for up to five days. If making pasta sheets, place two sheets on the pan and cover it with plastic wrap; layer another two sheets of pasta and cover that with wrap as well. Repeat until you have rolled all the dough out. Then wrap the entire pan tightly with plastic and refrigerate for up to four days.

Fresh pasta, because it already contains moisture, weighs twice as much as the same volume of dried pasta. That means that for a recipe calling for eight ounces of dried spaghetti, you would use sixteen ounces of fresh.

The Pasta Machine

For your gluten-free pasta, you should have a dedicated rolling machine that is never used for anything but gluten-free pasta. There are nooks and crannies in the rollers that could hide gluten-containing flour, so don't risk it.

After much practice, I can share some tips for using a pasta-rolling machine. I have a basic, ancient one, made of chromed steel and with a clamp that locks it to the table and a spaghetti-cutting attachment. It came with a ravioli attachment that I've found to be a frustrating waste of time, to be honest, so I just make ravioli by hand. The ravioli device does not work with the softer, less stretchy gluten-free dough, in my experience.

As with hand rolling, you need to use copious amounts of starch to keep the dough from sticking to the counter or to the rollers. Starting with your four-ounce portions of dough, flatten each with your palms or with a rolling pin on the counter, keeping an even and rectangular form about three to four inches wide. The dough should be ¼- to ⅓-inch thick to go through the rollers. Press any cracks or uneven pieces back into a nice even shape. Press the leading edge until it is very thin, which will make it easier to feed into the machine.

My machine, like most of them, has a wheel that you turn to open and close the roller, making a thicker or thinner sheet as desired. On my machine, #1 is the thickest setting, and #6 is paper thin. Set the thickness gauge at #1 (or whatever your machine's thickest setting is), and sprinkle the rollers with starch. Feed the dough through the rollers, supporting it as it comes out with your free hand. You will get a thick sheet of pasta. Turn the wheel to #2, and sprinkle the rollers with more starch. Feed the pasta through again. It will emerge in a long, thinner sheet. At this point, I recommend that you place the sheet of pasta on the counter (make sure there is still enough starch to keep it from sticking) and cut it in half crosswise so it will be easier to handle. Then sprinkle more starch on the rollers and feed each piece through on #3. Keep turning the knob, sprinkling the rollers with starch, and rolling the sheets through until you make a pass on the #4 or #5 setting. This is as thin as you can go, and it produces a sheet about 1/16-inch thick.

At this point, you can make noodles of varying widths or lasagna sheets. For spaghetti, linguine, or pappardelle, switch to the appropriate cutter, dust the pasta sheet with starch, and roll the sheets through, tossing the results with more starch. Form your pasta into a four-ounce pile, put it in a storage container, and cover it while you continue forming the rest of your pasta. Once all the pasta is rolled and cut, place some plastic wrap loosely over the portions of noodles in the container and cover tightly. This will keep for four to five days in the refrigerator.

For lasagna sheets, roll the dough through the rollers in the same manner and finish on the #5 setting. Each two-ounce piece should make a sheet of pasta about five inches wide and fifteen inches long. Dust a sheet pan with starch and layer the lasagna sheets with plastic wrap as described above for hand-rolled pasta sheets. Store in the refrigerator for up to four days.

Pasta Alternatives

With the many dietary concerns that diners have today, even gluten-free pasta may be a no-no. It still contains grain, starch, and carbohydrates, and while some of us love those features, others do not. For the low-carb diner, there are still some fun options to try.

Vegetable Noodles, Raw or Cooked

The original veggie noodle is made of spaghetti squash. Spaghetti squash grows a little pack of noodles inside it, just waiting for you to bake it and scoop the noodles out. Transforming other vegetables into strands that mimic pasta is a fun trick, too. At its most basic, a simple vegetable peeler can be used to shave thin strips, which can

be served raw or heated in a sauce. This is a fine way to introduce your palate to the wonders of zucchini, yellow squash, carrot, and parsnip linguine. Simply start peeling, turning the veggie as you go, until you reach the seedy or woody core, which you can discard.

If you like veggie noodles, you may want to explore some tool upgrades that will give you more options than a peeler can. For more impressive, consistently shaped noodles, you need a mandoline or slicer box or a spiral vegetable cutter. A mandoline is a handy tool that chefs use to make perfect slices of hard-to-cut vegetables quickly. For our purposes, you will use a julienne blade, which should come with the mandoline. Basically, you will push your vegetable across a set of blades that will cut it into even, linguine-sized slices. You can use it to cut vegetables such as potatoes, zucchini, and eggplant into perfect, thin slices. A spiral cutter is used to make curly strips of vegetables, of varying thicknesses. I found an inexpensive one that came with three blades for cutting different thicknesses. Using the spiral cutter, you impale the vegetable at one end and turn a handle at the other end, which rotates the vegetable while forcing it through the cutter. The resulting curls can be used in raw or cooked pasta preparations.

The main vegetables that I use for mandolined or spiral-cut noodles in this book are zucchini, yellow squash, carrots, parsnips, and white sweet potatoes. Zucchini is a good choice because it is easy to cut and is not a starchy vegetable. It's popular for raw dishes because you need only toss it with a little salt and olive oil and let it stand for a few minutes to soften. The one drawback is that if you have leftover zucchini noodles in sauce, the zucchini will weep liquids in the refrigerator overnight, softening in texture and diluting the sauce. Raw strands are best served very fresh.

To serve zucchini as a cooked pasta, I've experimented with boiling it and have found that it is so high in moisture that it becomes soggy. For best results with zucchini or squash noodles in cooked dishes, simply heat the noodles in the sauce or some oil just until warmed. This way they hold their liquids and soften just enough to become the texture of pasta.

Carrots can be prepared raw in the same manner as raw zucchini noodles. Combine the two for a colorful medley. Carrots can also be lightly cooked. White sweet potatoes and parsnips are sturdier vegetables good for shaping into pasta. A big sweet potato can yield a pasta strand almost as long as a piece of spaghetti. When mandolined into strips the width of fettuccine, sweet potatoes can be boiled for a couple of minutes to make a lovely al dente "pasta." Parsnips can be peeled in long strips as well, and they make good "orzo" when shredded.

Other veggies that can stand in for pasta include cabbage, which you can slice thinly and substitute for some or all of the noodles in a sauté or stir-fry. This is a great way to make pad thai or other noodle dishes with fewer carbs. Slivered collards and kale are not very convincing as pasta, but they can bulk up a dish like the Spicy Almond Collard Green "Noodles" with Cucumber (page 96).

Veggie "Pastas"

3 pounds spaghetti squash make 3 cups strands (will vary widely)

> 4 ounces spaghetti squash strands (about 1 cup cooked): 36 calories, 8 g carbohydrate

1½ pounds white sweet potatoes, trimmed and mandolined into linguine, make 6 cups cooked strands

> 4 ounces sweet potato strands (1 cup cooked): 96 calories, 24 g carbohydrate

1 pound parsnips, stripped with a peeler, makes 6 cups raw or 4 cups cooked strands

> 4 ounces parsnip strands (about 1 cup cooked): 80 calories, 20 g carbohydrate

1 pound carrots, stripped with a peeler, makes 6 cups raw or 4 cups cooked strands

> 4 ounces carrot strands (about 1 cup cooked): 44 calories, 12 g carbohydrate (376% DV of vitamin A, 12% DV vitamin C)

1 pound zucchini, stripped with a peeler, spiral-cut, or mandolined, makes 6 cups raw (which will shrink slightly as they soften in the marinade or sauce)

> 1 cup zucchini strands: 16 calories, 4 g carbohydrate (24% DV vitamin C)

2½ pounds zucchini, sliced ¼ inch thick and roasted on an oiled sheet pan for 8 to 10 minutes, will replace noodles in a 13 x 9-inch lasagna

> 3 ounces zucchini: 12 calories, 3 g carbohydrate

1 pound collard greens, slivered thinly, makes 6 cups raw (which will shrink to 4 cups when massaged with sauce)

> 4 ounces (about 1 cup after massaging): 36 calories, 8 g carbohydrate, 4 g protein (148% DV vitamin A, 64% DV vitamin C, 16% DV calcium)

1 pound cabbage, thinly slivered, makes 8 cups raw or 4 cups sautéed

> 2 ounces cabbage slivers (about 1 cup raw): 16 calories, 4 g carbohydrate (48 % DV vitamin C, 4% DV calcium, 2% DV vitamin A and 2% DV iron)

Other Low-Carb Options

Looking for more protein? Egg crêpes are the answer if you want to enjoy spaghetti without any carbs. You have the option of whisking in Parmesan cheese or garbanzo flour to make crêpes that can be sliced into noodles of varying widths. Egg crêpes can also be used as wrappers for foods like the Egg Crêpe Sushi with Smoked Salmon, Daikon, Carrots, and Wasabi Mayo (page 62), or to make cannelloni (page 174). Egg crêpes have the advantage of being a little more absorbent, so they quickly marry well with a sauce in the pan.

The other low- or no-carb option: shirataki noodles. Many grocery stores carry them, sometimes in the refrigerated section and sometimes on the shelf. They are made with konjac, yam, or tofu, so read the labels if you are avoiding any of those ingredients. Shirataki noodles come packed in water, and they just need to be drained and rinsed well. Sometimes they are very long, so I snip them with kitchen scissors in the strainer before adding to the dish.

With so many options to choose from, you are about to have a great adventure with gluten-free pastas!

BASIC FRESH PASTA

This fresh pasta is eggy and supple, like the fresh pasta you remember. It's a treat, whether tossed with a simple sauce, layered into lasagna, or rolled into cannelloni. Finely powdered whey adds protein, which gives the dough some strength in the absence of gluten. It's important that you weigh the flours, but if you choose to measure by volume, add the water gradually, just until a firm dough forms.

SERVES 4

¾ cup (90 grams) arrowroot starch

½ cup (60 grams) tapioca flour

½ cup (80 grams) sweet rice flour

⅓ cup (48 grams) millet flour

3 tablespoons whey protein powder (substitute ¾ cup/53 grams nonfat dry milk)

1 tablespoon guar gum

1 teaspoon xanthan gum

½ teaspoon fine salt

3 large eggs

3 to 4 tablespoons (44 to 60 milliliters) water

Measure the arrowroot starch, tapioca flour, sweet rice flour, millet flour, whey protein, guar gum, xanthan gum, and salt into the bowl of a stand mixer fitted with the dough hook, or a food processor. In a large measuring cup, whisk the eggs with 3 tablespoons of the water and add to the dry ingredients. Mix on low until the dough starts to come together. Turn off the mixer and press the dough together. You may have to sprinkle in some of the remaining tablespoon of water to moisten all the flour. Turn up the speed and beat for 2 minutes. In the processor, the machine will start to labor when the dough gets stiff, so take the dough out, place it on a starch-dusted countertop, and knead it manually for 2 to 3 minutes, until smooth and flexible.

Divide the dough into four 4-ounce portions, wrap the portions you are not using with plastic wrap, and either roll the dough out with a rolling pin on the counter or in a pasta-rolling machine (see page 24). Repeat with the remaining portions of dough. Leave as lasagna sheets or cut into noodles.

Bring a large pot of salted water to a boil for the pasta. Cook the noodles for 1½ to 2 minutes, then test. They should be tender but firm, just a little softer than al dente dried pasta. Drain and rinse well with warm water if serving warm, or cold water if serving cold, and serve immediately.

BUCKWHEAT PASTA

Buckwheat is a healthy whole grain, and it makes a dramatic, dark pasta. Soba is the most well-known form. You can make buckwheat noodles that go with both Asian and Italian flavors. Use it for the Tofu, Shiitake, and Water Chestnut Pot Stickers (page 78) or the Maltagliati with Chard, Lentils, and Smoked Paprika (page 126).

SERVES 4

½ cup (60 grams) arrowroot starch, plus more as needed for rolling

½ cup (60 grams) tapioca flour, plus more as needed for rolling

¾ cup (115 grams) buckwheat flour

¼ cup (40 grams) sweet rice flour

3 tablespoons whey protein powder (substitute ¾ cup/53 grams nonfat dry milk)

1 tablespoon guar gum

1 teaspoon xanthan gum

1 teaspoon fine salt

3 large eggs

3 to 4 tablespoons (44 to 60 milliliters) water

Measure the arrowroot starch, tapioca flour, buckwheat flour, sweet rice flour, whey protein powder, guar gum, xanthan gum, and salt into the bowl of a stand mixer fitted with the dough hook, or a food processor bowl. In a large measuring cup, whisk the eggs with 3 tablespoons of the water and add to the dry ingredients. Mix on low until the dough starts to come together. Turn off the mixer and press the dough together, you may have to sprinkle in some of the remaining tablespoon of water to moisten all the flour. Beat the mixture on high for another 2 minutes. The dough should be smooth and flexible. On a counter dusted with tapioca or arrowroot, press the dough into a ¾ inch thick rectangle and cut it into four 4-ounce pieces. Coat them liberally with starch, and put them in a resealable plastic bag or a sealed container to rest for at least 30 minutes at room temperature and up to 24 hours refrigerated.

Roll out each piece of dough with a rolling pin on the counter or in a pasta-rolling machine (see page 24). Leave as lasagna sheets or cut into noodles.

Bring a large pot of salted water to a boil for the pasta. Cook the noodles for 2 minutes, or longer if they were rolled by hand and are thicker than setting #5 (1/16 inch thick). They should be tender but firm to the bite, just slightly softer than al dente dried pasta.

EASY SPAETZLE

Spaetzle is a German tradition, often boiled in chicken stock and then drenched in butter as a side to schnitzel or wurst. It's an easy technique. A simple dough is mixed and grated to make rustic chunks of noodle that have lots of rough textures to hold sauce. Don't worry about how it looks: curly, flat, or lumpy, this easy spaetzel tastes great, despite having a homely appearance. You can use spaetzle as you would egg noodles, in soups and casseroles or as a base for saucy stews. Try it in the Spaetzle Chicken Soup with Carrots (page 201).

SERVES 4 TO 6

½ cup (80 grams) potato starch, plus more for handling

¼ cup (32 grams) corn flour

½ cup (60 grams) garbanzo flour

2 tablespoons whey protein powder

1 teaspoon fine salt

1 teaspoon guar gum

2 large eggs

6 cups water or chicken stock (optional)

In a food processor or large bowl, combine the potato starch, corn flour, garbanzo flour, whey protein powder, salt, and guar gum and pulse to mix. Add the eggs and process or stir to mix well. Scrape the dough onto a potato starch–dusted counter, and knead it for a couple of minutes. It will become firmer as the gum is activated. Bring a large pot of salted water or chicken stock to a boil for the spaetzle.

Place a box grater over the work surface or a large plate. Gather handfuls of dough and rub them across the large holes of the grater to shred the dough into pieces. If the shreds get long, cut them off with a knife and lightly dust them with starch so they won't stick together. Spread the pieces of dough out and dust them with starch as you add more.

Drop half of the grated dough into the boiling liquid and stir. When the spaetzle floats to the top of the pot and bobs on the surface, continue cooking for about another minute. Use a spider strainer or a slotted spoon to fish out the spaetzle, and drain it in a colander. Don't rinse, but toss it to keep it from sticking together. Cook the remaining spaetzle.

Add to soups or stews or simply toss with butter and flat-leaf parsley. Serve hot.

POTATO GNOCCHI

Potato gnocchi is the ultimate comfort food, with a pillowy, tender texture and a shape that begs to be drenched in sauce. These are so similar to regular wheat flour gnocchi that even Italians will never know that they are gluten-free.

SERVES 4 TO 6

1 pound Yukon gold potatoes, boiled whole, then slipped from their skins

¼ cup (30 grams) garbanzo flour

½ cup (80 grams) potato starch, plus more for shaping

¼ cup finely shredded Parmesan cheese, plus more for serving

1 pinch freshly grated nutmeg

2 large egg yolks

½ teaspoon fine salt

Olive oil, for drizzling

Put the warm potatoes through a potato ricer or mash them thoroughly. Let the potatoes cool completely. Directly on the counter, mix the potatoes, garbanzo flour, potato starch, Parmesan, nutmeg, egg yolks, and salt. Knead the mixture to make a very soft, but not sticky, dough. If it is sticky, knead in more starch, a little at a time, just until the dough isn't sticking to your fingers. Dust the counter with potato starch. Divide the dough into 4 pieces and roll them out in long cylinders about as thick as your finger. Cut the cylinders into ½-inch segments, and then press each segment gently against the tines of a fork to make the characteristic ribbed shape. If you are in a hurry, you can skip the fork step. Put the cut gnocchi on a sheet pan dusted with potato starch. Cover with plastic wrap and refrigerate until ready to cook.

Bring a large pot of salted water to a boil for the gnocchi. Drop a quarter of the gnocchi at a time into the boiling water. As the gnocchi come to the surface, transfer them with a slotted spoon or a spider strainer to a colander. Drizzle with oil and toss gently to keep them from sticking together. When all the gnocchi are cooked, add them to sauce and toss, or put the gnocchi on a platter and pour sauce over them. Pass Parmesan to sprinkle at serving.

HERBED SQUASH-FILLED RAVIOLI PILLOWS

As long as you are making ravioli, you might as well make a deeply savory, vegetable-rich filling. Your ravioli pillows will be more memorable that way. This method is a little easier; just fold the dough across the filling and seal three sides. The resulting filled pastas are plump and delicious. They need little more than garlic and olive oil, or the Creamy Cheese Sauce (page 45).

SERVES 4

2 pounds winter squash, preferably kabocha, red kuri, or buttercup
  baked and seeded

1 tablespoon extra-virgin olive oil, plus more for drizzling

2 packed tablespoons chopped fresh sage

2 garlic cloves, chopped

1 teaspoon fine salt

½ teaspoon cracked black pepper

½ cup ricotta cheese

½ cup shredded Parmesan cheese

1 large egg

1 recipe Basic Fresh Pasta (page 29)

Arrowroot starch, for dusting

Remove the skin from the baked squash and discard. Purée the squash and measure out 2 cups (reserve any leftovers for another use).

Heat the olive oil in a large sauté pan, then add the sage and garlic and cook over medium heat, just until the sage sizzles and the garlic is fragrant, about 2 minutes. Add the squash and cook, stirring, over medium heat for about 5 minutes, to thicken it. It should be almost as thick as canned pumpkin (the cooking time will depend on how moist your squash is). Take off the heat and transfer the squash mixture to a large bowl to cool. Stir in the salt and pepper.

When cooled to room temperature, stir in the ricotta, Parmesan, and egg.

Roll out the pasta dough to the #5 setting, 1/16 inch thick (see page 24), to make 4 long sheets. Dust your work surface with arrowroot and spread the sheets flat across it. Dust a sheet pan liberally with arrowroot. For a rustic, easy method, place tablespoon-size measures of filling on the lower half of the pasta sheet with 2 inches of space between them. Brush cool water on the pasta between the portions of filling, then carefully fold the top half of the dough over. Starting at one end, carefully press the dough around the filling, trying to avoid enclosing too much air. Press firmly to seal, then use a fluted wheel, pizza wheel, or knife to cut between the mounds of filling. Use a metal spatula to transfer the finished ravioli to the prepared sheet pan (they shouldn't touch or overlap). Put a piece of plastic wrap over the tray, and continue making the ravioli, placing them gently on the plastic wrap. Cover the finished tray with plastic wrap. The ravioli can be kept in the refrigerator for 2 days, tightly wrapped.

Bring a large pot of salted water to a boil for the pasta. Drop several ravioli into the boiling water and cook for about 4 minutes. Use a slotted spoon or strainer to scoop the ravioli out, place them in a colander, and drizzle them with olive oil. Shake the colander to coat them all evenly. Continue cooking the remaining ravioli, and transfer them from the colander to a casserole dish and keep warm. Serve with desired sauce and cheese.

SPINACH AND CHÈVRE-FILLED JUMBO TORTELLINI

Handmade tortellini takes some time and patience, but the resulting dish is so splendid that it's worth the effort. Use a 3½-inch metal biscuit cutter to make even circles of pasta. The creamy tanginess of chèvre gives the spinach a richness you don't find in standard ricotta fillings. Try these with Creamy Vodka Sauce (page 54). When cutting out circles for the tortellini, you will have some scraps of pasta leftover. Make sure to save them for later use.

SERVES 4

1 recipe Basic Fresh Pasta (page 29)

Starch, for dusting and rolling

8 ounces spinach, stems removed (not necessary if it's bagged baby spinach)

6 ounces chèvre cheese

½ cup grated Parmesan cheese

¼ teaspoon freshly grated nutmeg

½ teaspoon freshly grated lemon zest

¼ teaspoon fine salt

Using a pasta-rolling machine or a rolling pin, roll the pasta dough out to ¹⁄₁₆-inch thick (setting #5). Place the 4 pasta sheets on a starch-dusted sheet pan and cover tightly with plastic wrap, as described on page 25, until ready to use. Dust another pan with starch for holding the finished tortellini.

For the filling, bring a large pot of water to a boil, then drop in the spinach leaves. Stir and return to a boil, blanching until the leaves are just bright green, about 2 minutes. Drain the spinach and rinse with cold water. Wrap the spinach in a kitchen towel and wring it out to get the leaves bone dry, then chop the spinach and measure out ½ cup. In a medium bowl, combine the chèvre and Parmesan and mash until thoroughly mixed. Then mash in the spinach, nutmeg, zest, and salt Transfer the filling to a smaller bowl, and cover and chill until ready to use.

Set up a pastry brush and a cup with some water in it for brushing the pasta later. Place a sheet of pasta on a starch-dusted counter and cut out 3½-inch circles with a biscuit cutter, making sure to yield as many rounds as possible. On each round, place a scant tablespoon of filling, shaped to be slightly oval. Brush one side of the round with water, then fold the pasta over the filling and press to seal. Cradling the filled pasta and working gently to keep it from tearing, dampen one corner and bring the other corner to meet it; pinch to seal. This will form a tortellini shape. Continue forming the tortellini until all the dough and filling is used up. Place each tortellini on the starch-dusted pan and cover tightly with plastic wrap. The tortellini can be refrigerated for up to 24 hours.

Bring a large pot of salted water to a boil for the pasta. Drop in all of the tortellini and return to a boil, then reduce the heat to simmer gently. Cook for 3 to 4 minutes. Test by removing one with a slotted spoon or strainer and cutting it in half: the filling should be hot and melty, and the pasta should be tender. Drain, rinse with warm water, and serve with sauce.

NOTE: The pasta scraps can be rerolled for another pasta dish. Put the scraps in a food processor, sprinkle them with a teaspoon or two of water, and pulse to break them up. When the mixture looks like very coarse meal, squeeze a portion to see if it holds together. If necessary, add more water. When the dough can be pressed into a ball, take it out and roll it out again for noodles; use within about 4 days.

EGG CRÊPE "NOODLES"

If you don't have a pasta-rolling machine, or if you just really love eggs, these crêpes are a fun alternative to pasta. They can serve as savory wrappers for baked cannelloni, or they can be slivered to stand in for spaghetti. The resulting "noodles" will be more absorbent than your average pasta, and they will drink in a flavorful sauce. Try them with the Creamy Roasted Garlic and Mushroom Sauce (page 46) or with Bolognese (page 134).

SERVES 4 TO 6

½ cup (60 grams) garbanzo flour

¾ cup milk

1 teaspoon fine salt

8 large eggs, whisked

Canola oil, for the pan

Whisk the garbanzo flour, milk, and salt in a large bowl until smooth. Add the eggs and whisk again.

Heat an 8-inch crêpe pan or a small sauté pan over medium-high heat. Brush or spray with oil. Measure ¼ cup of crêpe batter into the pan and quickly swirl to coat just the bottom of the pan. Cook for a minute or two, until set and flip over carefully. Cook the second side for only a couple of seconds and transfer the crêpe to a cutting board to cool. Continue with the remaining crêpe batter.

When all the crêpes are cooked and cooled to room temperature, you can either use them for cannelloni or roll them up and slice them thinly into strands. Toss to fluff. These can be stored, tightly covered, for up to 4 days.

VEGGIE "NOODLE" BASICS

For a light, all-veggie option, try a vegetable noodle. Raw foodists may have pioneered the use of veggies as pasta, but we can all take a page from the raw food book and enjoy raw squash strands. You may also cook your veggie noodles for a low-carb, low-calorie base for the sauce of your choice. Veggie Spaghetti Sauce (page 43) and Spicy African Peanut Sauce (page 48) are great sauces to try on your veggie noodles.

These measurements are approximate. Older vegetables will yield less, as will ones that need trimming because they won't fit easily on the spiral cutter. When cutting zucchini and squash, you will end up discarding the center core of seeds, although if you use small, young squash, you can use it all. Parsnips and carrots, when done with the peeler, will also leave you with a core.

For spaghetti squash, preheat the oven to 400°F. Oil a sheet pan with olive oil. Cut the squash in half lengthwise and scoop out the seeds, discarding them. Place the squash cut-side down on the pan and roast for 30 to 40 minutes. Test the squash by turning a piece over and seeing whether the strands come apart easily when separated with a fork. If you test by piercing the skin of the squash, it is easy to overbake, which makes the results mushy. Cool the squash cut-side up on racks, then scoop out the strands. Separate and fluff them with a fork.

For sweet potatoes, parsnips, and carrots, use a spiral cutter, mandoline with a fine julienne blade, or peeler. Make long, thin "noodles," then drop them in boiling, salted water for about 1 to 2 minutes, depending on the size of your strands. Test at 2 minutes; a few of the noodles will just start to break apart when they are done. Drain and gently rinse.

SERVES 4

START WITH ONE OF THE FOLLOWING VEGETABLES:

2 pounds spaghetti squash

1 pound white sweet potatoes, peeled

1 pound parsnips, peeled

1 pound carrots, peeled

1 pound zucchini

1 pound yellow squash

For parsnips and carrots, pat dry. Parsnips and carrots are sturdy enough to simmer in a sauce for a few minutes, if desired.

For zucchini or yellow squash, or a combination of the two, use a spiral cutter, mandoline with a fine julienne blade, or peeler. Make long, thin "noodles," and toss them with a pinch of salt and a dash of olive oil. Let them sit for 20 to 30 minutes at room temperature to release moisture and soften, and then drain and toss with sauce. For warm preparations, make the sauce and heat it in a wide sauté pan over medium heat, then add the veggie strands and toss, just until the strands are warmed and softened. Don't overcook or the noodles will become soggy.

Ahhh, spaghetti. Drenched in red gravy, perhaps topped with a couple of meatballs and some Parmesan cheese. It's the iconic Southern Italian-American food that many of us grew up with. The first waves of Italians who came to America and opened restaurants were from Southern Italy, where tomato sauce is king. They introduced us to lasagna, manicotti, and jugs of cheap red wine. We couldn't get enough, and all these foods are now as much a part of American cuisine as apple pie and hot dogs. We love our tomato sauces and have come up with infinite variations on the theme. I've included a classic Bolognese and a veggie sauce for anyone looking to share pasta with a vegetarian.

But our dining has become far more global in recent times. Tomato sauces are glorious, but so are creamy sauces, roasted vegetable purées, nut-based sauces, and even raw veggie sauces. Luckily, all of these options can easily be made gluten-free. The Creamy Cheese Sauce (page 45) and Creamy Roasted Garlic and Mushroom Sauce (page 46) take two different approaches in the making of white sauces. One uses a gluten-free flour roux and the other a simple reduction of cream. Either way, you get the rich, comforting pasta sauce that you crave.

Travel the globe and try the Spicy African Peanut Sauce (page 48) on noodles or on the sweet potato shreds in the recipe on page 140. A veggie delight is born in the Curried Veggie Purée (page 51) when it is tossed with noodles. The creaminess of the eggplant and other veggies makes the sauce really satisfying.

Don't hold yourself back. Try the Raw Tomato–Avocado Sauce with Zucchini Noodles (page 53), especially on a hot summer day. It's a no-cook recipe, and the light, refreshing dish may surprise you.

How Much Sauce?

Classic Italian technique states that 1½ cups chunky tomato sauce or 1 cup pesto-type sauce per pound of dried pasta is the perfect ratio. I don't think there is anything wrong with ladling on a little more, especially when the sauce is loaded with vegetables. It helps, too, to make your gluten-free pasta alternative seem more like your favorite and familiar wheat pasta. On the other hand, if the sauce is very rich, you may want to apply it sparingly, using just enough to moisten your pasta or noodles and veggies.

So feel free to "drown" your pasta in veggies and sauce. I've used up to four or five cups of thick and chunky Veggie Spaghetti Sauce (page 43) or Veggie Beef Tomato Sauce with Red Bell Peppers (page 44) on one pound of spaghetti, penne, or shells.

When saucing your pasta, use the absorbency of gluten-free pasta to your advantage. Heat your sauce in a wide sauté pan or pot, so it will be nice and hot when the pasta is done. Then cook the pasta to nearly al dente and reserve a few tablespoons of the cooking water. Drain the pasta, rinse with hot water, and drain again. Then dump the hot pasta into the hot sauce and use tongs or two wooden spoons to toss the pasta in the sauce, heating it and finishing the cooking for a minute or so. If the sauce seems too thick, stir in about a tablespoon of the reserved cooking water. This technique works with all of these sauces, and it is a good way to soften raw zucchini noodles in sauce, just briefly, before serving.

Pasta Shapes to Pair with Sauces

The many shapes of pasta add infinite variety to what is really the same basic dish. Lasagna is for layering and baking, jumbo shells are for stuffing, and slender spaghetti and linguine are for tossing in lighter sauces. Therefore, you can take my pasta shape recommendations with a grain of salt and feel free to do whatever you want.

For thick and chunky sauces, pastas with lots of texture and crevices to help hold nubbins of beef or carrot are always recommended. Penne, shells, campanelle, fusilli, pagodas, and other structurally shaped pastas hold up well in the heavy sauces, and they are great in baked dishes, holding their shapes and providing fork-able, bite-size portions.

For thinner sauces that are either cream-based or pesto style, long pastas like spaghetti, linguine, and fettuccine are often de rigueur. That being said, who hasn't enjoyed spaghetti with meat sauce or a penne dish tossed in creamy sauce or pesto?

In general, Asian soy sauce–based sauces, nut- and seed-based sauces, and coconut curries are best with long noodles or pasta, although nobody will stop you from enjoying a dish of rotini in Szechuan Sesame Sauce (page 47).

Veggie Spaghetti Sauce • 43

Veggie Beef Tomato Sauce with Red Bell Pepper • 44

Creamy Cheese Sauce • 45

Creamy Roasted Garlic and Mushroom Sauce • 46

Szechuan Sesame Sauce • 47

Spicy African Peanut Sauce • 48

Red Curry Sauce • 50

Curried Veggie Purée • 51

Raw Tomato–Avocado Sauce with Zucchini Noodles • 53

Creamy Vodka Sauce • 54

Salsa di Oliva Nera • 55

VEGGIE SPAGHETTI SAUCE

This is a simple sauce to use for everything. It is full of chunky vegetables but is delicious and tomatoey enough that kids love it. Make a double batch to freeze and use it for quick weeknight spaghetti, pizzas, and lasagna, or anywhere else a red sauce would be appropriate. I use Muir Glen canned tomatoes.

SERVES 6 (MAKES 6 CUPS)

2 tablespoons extra-virgin olive oil

2 large yellow onions, chopped

1 pinch red pepper flakes (optional)

4 garlic cloves, minced

4 ribs celery, diced

2 large carrots, diced

2 tablespoons fresh thyme leaves, coarsely chopped

¼ cup red wine (dry Burgundy or chianti)

1 (15-ounce) can tomato sauce

1 (15-ounce) can tomato purée

1 (14.5-ounce) can diced tomatoes

1 teaspoon fine salt, plus more as needed

Freshly ground black pepper

In a 4-quart pot, heat the olive oil over medium-high heat. Add the onion, pepper flakes, garlic, celery, carrot, and thyme. Once the mixture begins to sizzle, reduce the heat to medium-low. Cook, stirring often, for at least 10 minutes, and up to an hour if you have the time, to caramelize the onions and add more depth of flavor. Add the wine and bring to a boil, then stir in the tomato sauce and purée, diced tomatoes, salt, and pepper.

Bring the mixture to a boil, then reduce the heat to a simmer and cook for about 15 to 20 minutes, or until the sauce is thick and the vegetables are very tender. Season with more salt and pepper, if desired.

VEGGIE BEEF TOMATO SAUCE
WITH RED BELL PEPPER

Hearty beef gets a little boost from meaty mushrooms, making this sauce seem meatier than it really is. A symphony of colorful, tasty veggies perks up the palate and makes sweet music with the tangy tomatoes.

SERVES 6 (MAKES 6 CUPS)

1 tablespoon extra-virgin olive oil

1 medium onion, chopped

1 rib celery, chopped

1 small carrot, chopped

3 garlic cloves, chopped

1 small zucchini, quartered and sliced

2 cups button mushrooms, chopped

1 pound ground beef

½ teaspoon fine salt

Freshly ground black pepper

1 (28-ounce) can whole tomatoes, crushed

1 large red bell pepper, chopped

2 tablespoons fresh thyme leaves, chopped

In a large pot, heat the olive oil over medium-high heat and add the onion, celery, and carrot. Sauté over medium heat until the onions are translucent, about 5 minutes. Add the garlic, zucchini, and mushrooms and sauté for 5 minutes, or until the vegetables start to brown. Add the beef and raise the heat to high, crumbling the beef with a wooden spoon as it cooks. Add the salt and pepper.

When the beef is no longer pink, about 5 minutes, add the tomatoes, pepper, and thyme and bring the mixture to a boil. Simmer until thick, about 30 minutes.

Toss with the pasta of your choice or use for lasagna.

CREAMY CHEESE SAUCE

Lots of people crave creamy, rich foods, and GF diners can enjoy a creamy, cheesy sauce, thanks to this recipe. A simple roux of white rice flour and butter thickens the sauce a bit, and a judicious measure of cheese finishes the thickening while also adding cheesy goodness. This can easily be made with non-dairy alternatives for a vegan version.

SERVES 6 (MAKES 3 CUPS)

2 tablespoons unsalted butter

1 medium yellow onion, minced

3 tablespoons white rice flour

2¼ cups milk

½ teaspoon fine salt

½ teaspoon ground white pepper

1 cup shredded Parmesan or other aged cheese, such as Gruyère or Cheddar

Melt the butter in a 4-quart saucepan over medium heat. Add the onion and sauté until translucent, about 5 minutes. Stir in the rice flour, making sure you get it all worked into a paste. Cook for another 5 minutes, or until it starts to stick, stirring constantly. Take off the heat and pour in the milk gradually, whisking out the flour lumps. Stir in the salt and pepper and return to medium heat. Stir frequently until the mixture comes to a boil, then reduce the heat and stir for a few seconds more.

Take off the heat and add the cheese, stirring until it has completely melted. Serve warm with the pasta of your choice. Let the sauce cool to room temperature before refrigerating in a covered container for up to a week.

CREAMY ROASTED GARLIC
AND MUSHROOM SAUCE

If you don't feel completely comfortable making a roux, try this sauce. Deeply flavored with dried and fresh mushrooms and roasted garlic, it is made lush with just enough cream for that buttery texture you love.

SERVES 6 (MAKES 1½ CUPS)

1 head garlic

3 teaspoons extra-virgin olive oil, divided

8 ounces cremini or button mushrooms

1 cup boiling water

½ ounce dried mushrooms

½ cup dry white wine

½ cup heavy cream

½ cup packed fresh parsley leaves, chopped

½ teaspoon fine salt

Preheat the oven to 400°F. Slice off the top of the head of garlic and drizzle 1 teaspoon of oil over the tops of the cloves before wrapping the head in foil. Roast for 20 to 30 minutes, until the head is buttery soft when pierced with a paring knife.

Halve the fresh mushrooms and toss them with the remaining 2 teaspoons olive oil on a sheet pan. Roast for 20 to 30 minutes. The mushrooms will be shrunken and dark. Remove from the oven and set aside.

Meanwhile, pour the boiling water over the dried mushrooms in a glass measuring cup and let them hydrate until softened, about 40 minutes for whole mushrooms. Remove the rehydrated mushrooms, squeezing them over the cup to extract as much water as possible. Set the measuring cup aside to reserve the soaking water. Trim away the tough stems of the mushrooms and mince the caps.

Combine the minced rehydrated mushrooms with the white wine in a large sauté pan over high heat and bring to a boil. Boil, reducing the heat as necessary, until the wine is reduced by half. Add the cream and the reserved soaking water, pouring it in slowly to leave the grit behind in the measuring cup. Add the roasted mushrooms and bring the mixture back to a boil, then reduce to a vigorous simmer. Squeeze the roasted garlic pulp into a small bowl and mash it coarsely, then add it to the simmering sauce. Add the parsley and salt. Cook, stirring occasionally, for about 10 minutes, or until the sauce is thick enough to coat the back of a spoon. This sauce keeps, tightly covered, in the refrigerator for up to a week.

SZECHUAN SESAME SAUCE

For your dairy-free friends, serve this sauce as a celebration of the nutty, creamy joy that can be found in nut and seed butters. This is a great sub for those sesame noodles you used to get as Chinese takeout—just serve with the Cold Szechuan Noodles with Sriracha and Cucumbers (page 84). The added benefit is that you will have plenty of leftover sauce to use in other dishes as well. Salads, stir-fries, and even sandwiches are made irresistible with a dose of this tasty sauce.

SERVES 8 (MAKES 1³/₄ CUPS)

4 garlic cloves, peeled

2 tablespoons peeled and sliced fresh ginger

½ cup tahini

4 tablespoons smooth peanut butter

¼ cup brewed black tea, at room temperature

2 tablespoons toasted sesame oil

6 tablespoons wheat-free tamari

4 tablespoons rice vinegar

2 tablespoons packed light brown sugar

2 teaspoons Sriracha sauce

In a food processor or by hand, mince the garlic and ginger. Add the tahini and peanut butter and process or whisk in a bowl until smooth. Add the tea, sesame oil, tamari, rice vinegar, brown sugar and Sriracha and process or whisk until smooth. Use immediately, or refrigerate, tightly covered, for up to a week.

SPICY AFRICAN PEANUT SAUCE

The groundnut stews and *mafe* of Africa rely on the beloved peanut for extra protein, thickening, and that ever-popular flavor. With very little effort on your part, you can create a sauce that is a little spicy, bursting with complex flavor, and gluten-free. Use it in the White Sweet Potato Noodles with Collards on page 140.

SERVES 8 (MAKES 2 CUPS)

1 tablespoon extra-virgin olive oil

1 medium yellow onion, chopped

1 tablespoon minced fresh ginger

3 garlic cloves, chopped

1 teaspoon ground cumin

1 teaspoon ground coriander

½ teaspoon ground cinnamon

½ teaspoon red pepper flakes

½ cup crunchy peanut butter

1 cup vegetable or chicken stock

1 cup diced fresh tomato

1 tablespoon packed light brown sugar

½ teaspoon fine salt

1 tablespoon freshly squeezed lemon juice

In a 4-quart pot, heat the olive oil over medium-high heat for 1 minute. Add the onion and sauté until soft and translucent, about 5 minutes. Add the ginger, garlic, cumin, coriander, cinnamon, and pepper flakes and stir for a couple of minutes, until fragrant. In a medium bowl, whisk together the peanut butter and stock, then stir into the pot. Add the tomato, brown sugar, salt, and lemon and bring to a simmer. Cook over low heat for 5 minutes, or until slightly thickened.

Use this sauce with noodles (as on page 140), as a dipping sauce, or in sandwiches and wraps. It keeps, tightly covered, in the refrigerator for up to a week.

RED CURRY SAUCE

The Thai place you used to love puts wheat-based soy sauce in everything, so it is a great relief to find that the GF version of this sauce is really easy to make at home. A safe brand for curry paste is Thai Kitchen because they use no mystery ingredients.

SERVES 6 (MAKES 1¼ CUPS)

2 tablespoons red curry paste

1 (14-ounce) can coconut milk

2 garlic cloves, chopped

3 medium kaffir lime leaves or the zest of 1 lime, pared off in a ¾-inch-wide strip

2 tablespoons palm sugar or packed light brown sugar

2 tablespoons freshly squeezed lime juice

2 tablespoons fish sauce or wheat-free tamari

In a 2-quart saucepan off the heat, whisk together the red curry paste and the coconut milk until smooth. Add the garlic, lime leaves or zest, sugar, lime juice, and fish sauce or tamari and stir to combine. Bring to a boil over medium-high heat, then reduce the heat and simmer. Cook for about 5 minutes, or until just slightly thickened.

If you are using the sauce right away, simmer to the desired thickness, or use in the Red Curry Scallops and Sweet Potato with Rice Noodles (page 150). If you are reserving the sauce for another day, take it off the heat and let it stand for 10 minutes to cool and to infuse with flavor. Store, tightly covered, in the refrigerator for up to a week. In either case, remove the lime leaves or zest before serving.

CURRIED VEGGIE PURÉE

All sauces need something to give them body, so why not use vegetables and purée them into a creamy sauce? In this exotic sauce, Indian spices and creamy coconut milk combine with a garden harvest of veggies to give you plenty of flavors and textures that keep you entertained bite after bite!

SERVES 6 TO 8 (MAKES 3½ CUPS)

1 tablespoon canola oil or ghee

8 ounces eggplant, peeled and cubed

8 ounces zucchini, cubed

1 medium yellow onion, chopped

2 medium tomatoes, chopped

2 medium red jalapeños (or to taste), seeded and chopped

2 tablespoons minced fresh ginger

2 teaspoons whole brown mustard seeds

2 teaspoons ground coriander

2 teaspoons ground cumin

1 teaspoon ground turmeric

½ cup canned coconut milk

1 tablespoon freshly squeezed lemon juice

1 tablespoon honey

1 teaspoon fine salt

½ teaspoon freshly ground black pepper

Heat the oil or ghee briefly over medium-high heat and add the eggplant, zucchini, onion, tomatoes, and jalapeños. Cook, stirring occasionally, until the eggplant is tender and soft, about 10 minutes, lowering the heat to medium if it starts to stick to the pan. Add the ginger, mustard seeds, coriander, cumin, and turmeric, and stir over medium-high heat until fragrant, about 1 minute. Add the coconut milk and bring the mixture to a boil. Reduce the heat to medium and simmer for a couple of minutes, just to thicken it to the consistency of tomato sauce.

Measure 2 cups of the vegetable sauté and put it in a blender or food processor. Use a folded kitchen towel to hold the lid of the processor, to avoid being burned by the hot liquids, and purée until smooth. Return the purée to the pan and add the lemon and honey. Cook over medium heat for about 5 minutes, to thicken the sauce. Season with the salt and pepper. Adjust the seasonings to your liking. This can be stored, tightly covered, for up to a week in the refrigerator.

RAW TOMATO AVOCADO SAUCE WITH ZUCCHINI NOODLES

As long as we are exploring veggies as noodles, we might as well explore a raw version and see how you like it. In this quick and easy dish, chopped tomatoes and herbs combine with rich, creamy avocado for a pasta-like experience. But it is made using nothing but plants. This is such a tasty sauce, you may well want to toss it with cooked linguine, too. Eight ounces of dried linguine would stand in for the raw noodles.

SERVES 4 TO 6 (MAKES 2 CUPS)

1 pound zucchini

½ teaspoon plus a pinch fine salt, divided

¼ cup plus ½ teaspoon extra-virgin olive oil, divided

5 ounces whole cherry tomatoes

1 cup sun-dried tomatoes, soaked in cool water until soft

2 garlic cloves, pressed

½ cup packed fresh basil leaves, chopped

2 tablespoons packed fresh oregano, chopped

¼ cup minced yellow onion

1 teaspoon freshly grated lemon zest

1 tablespoon freshly squeezed lemon juice

1 large ripe avocado

Trim the stem and the blossom ends from the zucchini and discard. Then use a peeler or mandoline to make thin strips. Put the strips in a large bowl and sprinkle with a pinch of salt and ½ teaspoon of olive oil. Toss together to coat and let stand for 10 to 20 minutes.

Chop the cherry tomatoes and the rehydrated sun-dried tomatoes and combine in another large bowl. Add the remaining ¼ cup olive oil and ½ teaspoon salt, the garlic, basil, oregano, onion, lemon zest, and lemon juice and toss to mix. Just before serving, cut the avocado in half, remove the pit, and use a paring knife to cut the flesh into cubes in the shell. Then use a spoon to scoop out the cubed flesh into the bowl.

Gently toss the zucchini or pasta with the tomato mixture and the avocado and serve immediately.

CREAMY VODKA SAUCE

Vodka is the secret ingredient in this sauce: alcohol has the amazing ability to break out flavor compounds in tomatoes that can't be released any other way. Use a potato-based vodka such as Smirnoff or Chopin to avoid grain-based spirits. For a fun twist, I use crème fraîche instead of the usual cream, which adds a tangy richness and thickens the sauce beautifully.

SERVES 6 TO 8 (MAKES 3½ CUPS)

2 tablespoons extra-virgin olive oil

1 medium yellow onion, minced

3 garlic cloves, chopped

1 small carrot, chopped

2 (28-ounce) cans whole tomatoes, drained

1 cup potato-based vodka

1 teaspoon fine salt

½ cup crème fraîche

½ cup shredded Romano cheese

In an 8-quart pot, heat the olive oil over medium-high heat for a minute. Add the onion, garlic, and carrot and sauté until the onion is soft and golden, about 10 minutes. Add the whole tomatoes, crushing them roughly with your hands as you add each one. Add the vodka and salt and bring the mixture to a boil over high heat, then reduce the heat to a low simmer. Cook uncovered until the sauce is almost dry, about 30 minutes.

Purée the tomato mixture in a blender or food processor, or using a stick blender, being very careful when handling the hot liquid. When the mixture is smooth, add the crème fraîche and blend again to combine. Transfer the mixture back to the pot and heat it gently over medium-low heat until warm. Toss with hot pasta and the Romano. This sauce keeps, tightly covered, in the refrigerator for up to a week.

SALSA DI OLIVA NERA

This is a classic sauce from Southern Italy that has a few tweaks to make it easier in the American kitchen. It is perfect for raw zucchini pasta or quick spaghetti. Just a bit of chopping and you have a flavor-packed sauce with sweet, tangy, and herbal notes.

SERVES 4 TO 6 (MAKES 1 CUP)

½ cup pitted kalamata olives or Italian black olives, chopped

1 large Roma tomato, cored and chopped

2 garlic cloves, chopped

¼ cup packed fresh parsley leaves, chopped

2 tablespoons fresh thyme leaves, chopped

¼ cup golden raisins, coarsely chopped

1 teaspoon freshly grated orange zest

2 tablespoons freshly squeezed orange juice

¼ cup extra-virgin olive oil

½ teaspoon fine salt

On a cutting board, combine the chopped olives, tomato, garlic, parsley, and thyme. Mince it all together on the board to make a coarse paste. Transfer the olive mixture to a medium bowl and stir in the raisins, zest, juice, olive oil, and salt. Let stand at room temperature for at least half an hour, allowing the flavors to marry. This can be made a day or two ahead of time and refrigerated, covered, until you are ready to serve it.

APPETIZERS

Appetizers are all about fun. You can serve them at the start of a meal as a kind of teaser to give people a small, tasty bite before the main event. A great appetizer gets people excited and gives their palate a little sparkle before the next course. Apps can also be party food—the kind of noshable, appealing food that goes well with a glass of wine or beer. Little servings allow diners to try more than one and to eat in a free, pleasure-centric way.

Appetizers are often fraught with danger for GF diners. Bruschetta is made with wheaty baguettes, standard gluten-containing crackers surround the cheese, and your typical egg roll or dumpling is wrapped in a wheat-flour dough. But now, you can master some delicious apps that will please not just the GF eater but everyone else as well. Crab and mango spring rolls with a tasty burnt chile dipping sauce (page 65) will never be pegged as some kind of special diet food. Egg Crêpe Sushi with Smoked Salmon, Daikon, Carrots, and Wasabi Mayo (page 62) will entice sushi lovers and kids (who may not be too sure about it) equally. Steamed Shrimp Dumplings with Chile Dipping Sauce (page 76) and Tofu, Shiitake, and Water Chestnut Pot Stickers (page 78) are the ultimate finger food, and they make a great first course for a gluten-free crowd—who, I promise you, is missing dumplings.

Instead of bread-based appetizers, try the Roasted Red Pepper and Zucchini Involtini (page 70), which rolls up all those bruschetta flavors in the gentle embrace of roasted veggie slices. Avocado halves, stuffed with shrimp and noodle salad (page 71), are a welcome relief from crackers. And the pasta lover in you will devour Lasagna Rolls with Arrabbiata Sauce (page 68), an absolutely simple and easy nosh with a kicky sauce.

Your gluten-free appetizers will be the talk of the party, and they will become part of your food canon in no time.

CRISPY NOODLE CAKES
WITH **PEAS** AND **ORANGE-MISO TOFU**

Noodles are already incredibly appealing, but when you fry them in these crispy cakes, they become irresistible. You can make a lovely, single-serving presentation by forming them with a biscuit cutter or ring mold in the pan, or you can cook them more free-form—whatever suits you.

SERVES 8

½ recipe Basic Fresh Pasta (page 29), cut into thin spaghetti noodles

1 small carrot, finely diced

1 large egg

½ cup frozen green peas, thawed

⅛ teaspoon fine salt

¼ cup freshly squeezed orange juice

1 tablespoon chopped fresh ginger

2 tablespoons mirin

2 tablespoons red miso paste

1 teaspoon wheat-free tamari

6 tablespoons canola oil, divided

8 ounces extra-firm tofu, sliced into 8 pieces

4 medium scallions, slivered, for garnish

¼ cup black sesame seeds, for garnish

Bring a large pot of salted water to a boil for the pasta. Drop in the fresh noodles and the carrot and cook for 2 minutes, or until the pasta is tender and slightly chewy. Drain, don't rinse, and let cool slightly while you whisk the egg in a large bowl. Add the cooled pasta and carrot, peas, and salt to the egg and toss to mix. Set aside.

In a measuring cup, whisk together the orange juice, ginger, mirin, miso, and tamari.

In a large sauté pan, heat 2 tablespoons of the canola oil. Add the tofu slices in a single layer and sear on one side until browned, about 3 to 4 minutes. Turn the slices over and cook for a couple of minutes to sear the other side. Stir the orange juice mixture again to recombine and pour it over the tofu in the pan. Cook, basting and shaking the pan to keep the tofu from sticking, until the sauce thickens and the tofu is golden, about 2 to 4 minutes.

In another large sauté pan, heat the remaining 4 tablespoons of oil. Place a 3-inch biscuit cutter on a metal spatula and lightly pack in one-eighth of the noodle mixture, then slide the round out of the cutter into the hot oil in the pan. Cook on each side until crisp, about 2 minutes per side, adjusting the heat as necessary. Cook in batches, leaving room between the cakes so that they do not touch. Alternatively, you can make free-form cakes by carefully slipping ¼ to ½ cup of the noodle mixture into the oil. Cook for about 2 minutes on each side until crisp.

Serve each noodle cake topped with a slice of tofu and drizzled with the pan sauce. Garnish with scallions and sesame seeds.

CHINESE NOODLE SALAD
IN LETTUCE CUPS

Lettuce leaves form a light, crunchy little bowl for this tasty noodle salad, so you can eat it with your hands. They also stand in for gluten-containing wrappers, making this a perfect GF appetizer to take to a party and share.

SERVES 6

2 heads Bibb lettuce

2 cups shredded green cabbage

½ cup fresh cilantro leaves

4 scallions, slivered

1 small cucumber, seeded and chopped

2 tablespoons sesame oil

3 tablespoons wheat-free tamari

3 tablespoons rice vinegar

2 tablespoons honey or agave

6 ounces rice vermicelli

4 ounces chicken breast, cooked and shredded

GF hoisin sauce, for serving

Sriracha sauce, for serving

Sesame seeds, for serving

Cashews, for serving

Bring a large pot of salted water to a boil for the noodles.

Separate the lettuce leaves and wash them carefully; remove the tough base of each leaf. Spin dry or roll gently in kitchen towels and set aside.

In a large bowl, combine the cabbage, cilantro, scallions, and cucumber. Place the sesame oil, tamari, rice vinegar, and honey or agave in a measuring cup and whisk to mix.

Cook the noodles in the boiling water according to the package directions, drain, rinse with cold water, and drain again. Gently wrap the cooked noodles in a kitchen towel to dry them more completely. Transfer the noodles to the bowl with the cabbage mixture (some may stick to the towel, so just scrape them off as best you can). Drizzle with the sesame oil mixture and toss to coat. Add the chicken and toss again.

To serve, you have two options. You can portion the noodle salad into each lettuce leaf and place them on a tray, to serve as finger food. Or you can put the lettuce in a large bowl and the filling in another and have diners assemble their own. Set out the hoisin sauce, Sriracha, sesame seeds, and cashews for diners to use as desired.

EGG CRÊPE SUSHI WITH SMOKED SALMON, DAIKON, CARROTS, AND WASABI MAYO

When you are looking for an appetizer that doesn't rely on bread or crackers, you can try wrapping things in an egg crêpe. Egg crêpes can be customized to wrap just about anything. In this recipe, a sheet of nori is placed on the crêpe for a sushi flavor. If you are serving these to people who don't like nori, however, you can leave it out. The fluffy egg wrappers encase tasty rice, savory smoked salmon, and crisp veggies and may win over kids and picky eaters.

SERVES 6

1¼ cups water plus 2 tablespoons, divided

1 cup sushi rice

1 tablespoon rice vinegar

1 teaspoon granulated sugar

10 large eggs, lightly beaten

2 tablespoons mirin

1 teaspoon fine salt

Canola oil, for the pan

6 sheets nori

2 tablespoons mayonnaise

1 teaspoon wasabi paste, plus more for serving

6 ounces smoked salmon

12 long, thin slices daikon

12 long, thin slices carrot

Wheat-free tamari, for serving

Pickled ginger slices, for serving

Thirty minutes before making the crepes, put 1¼ cups of water and the sushi rice in a small saucepan with a tight-fitting lid and bring to a boil over medium-high heat. Reduce the heat to low, cover, and cook, undisturbed, about 14 minutes. The water should all be absorbed. Take off the heat and scrape the rice onto a plate to cool. In a small cup, stir the rice vinegar and sugar together until the sugar is dissolved and sprinkle it over the rice, folding it in with a rice paddle or spatula so that you don't break the grains. Cover with a damp towel and let it cool to room temperature while you prepare the crêpes.

Whisk the eggs with the mirin, salt, and remaining 2 tablespoons of water in a large bowl. Heat a 9-inch nonstick skillet over medium-high heat. Lightly oil the pan and pour in ⅓ cup of the egg mixture. Cook for 1 minute, until the bottom is set but the top is still moist. Place a nori sheet in the center of the crêpe and press down lightly. Cook for 30 seconds more, or until the top is set. Invert the pan over a sheet of waxed paper and gently shake the crêpe free to cool. Repeat to form the remaining egg crêpes.

In a small bowl, mix the mayonnaise and wasabi.

Transfer a few crepes onto a cutting board, nori-side up, and distribute a thin layer of rice over each nori sheet. Then place 1 ounce of the salmon and two slices each of daikon and carrot on each sheet, leaving a 1-inch border at the top. Smear a heaping teaspoon of wasabi mayonnaise across the salmon. Roll up each crêpe and place it seam-side down on a plate. Repeat with the remaining crêpes and cover tightly with plastic wrap. Refrigerate until ready to serve.

To serve, slice each roll into 6 pieces. If desired, you can insert toothpicks to hold the rounds together tightly, or just leave them seam-side down and let people pick them up. Offer small bowls of wheat-free tamari, dabs of wasabi, and pickled ginger alongside the sushi.

CURRY NOODLE AND PANEER CAKES WITH MANGO RAITA

These crispy, lightly spiced noodle cakes are studded with bits of cheese and topped with tangy mango raita. They make a wonderful first course and are a welcome change from the usual Indian appetizers.

SERVES 8

NOODLE CAKES

1 large egg, beaten

½ teaspoon curry powder

3 ounces paneer or halloumi, diced

⅛ teaspoon fine salt

½ recipe Basic Fresh Pasta (page 29), cut into linguine

Canola oil for frying

MANGO RAITA

1 tablespoon minced fresh ginger

1 cup diced fresh mango

1 cup plain yogurt

1 tablespoon brown mustard seeds

1 tablespoon cumin seeds

2 tablespoons light brown sugar

1 tablespoon freshly squeezed lemon juice

¼ cup packed fresh cilantro leaves, for garnish

Make the noodle cakes: Bring a large pot of salted water to a boil for the pasta. In a medium bowl, whisk the egg, curry powder, cheese, and salt. Cook the pasta in the boiling water for 2 minutes and drain but don't rinse. Let it cool for 1 minute, then toss with the egg mixture.

Make the mango raita: In a medium bowl, stir together the ginger, mango, and yogurt. In a small skillet over medium-high heat, toast the seeds until fragrant, 1 to 2 minutes, and stir into the yogurt mixture, then stir in the brown sugar and lemon juice.

In a large skillet, heat the oil. Place a 3-inch biscuit cutter on a metal spatula and lightly pack in one-eighth of the noodle mixture, then slide the round out of the cutter into the hot oil in the pan. Cook on each side until crisp, about 2 minutes per side, adjusting the heat as necessary. Cook in batches, leaving room between the cakes so they do not touch. Alternatively, you can make free-form cakes by carefully slipping ¼ to ½ cup of the noodle mixture into the oil. Cook for about 2 minutes on each side until crisp.

Serve each hot noodle cake topped with a dollop of raita. Garnish with cilantro.

MANGO CRAB SUMMER ROLLS WITH BURNT CHILE SAUCE

Summer rolls are the cool, light alternative to fried egg rolls, and they just happen to be easily made gluten-free. If crab is too pricey, feel free to substitute shrimp or tofu in its place.

SERVES 4 TO 8

SAUCE

½ cup canola oil

5 tablespoons slivered garlic

½ cup thinly sliced shallots

3 tablespoons red pepper flakes

¼ cup granulated sugar

2 teaspoons fine salt

ROLLS

1 pound king crab legs or 8 ounces picked-over crab meat

1 tablespoon fish sauce or wheat-free tamari

1 tablespoon granulated sugar

2 tablespoons freshly squeezed lemon juice

2 teaspoons cracked black pepper

4 ounces rice vermicelli

8 (8-inch) rice paper rounds

1 small English cucumber, cut into matchsticks

1 medium mango, cut into matchsticks

1 medium carrot, cut into matchsticks

½ cup cilantro sprigs

RECIPE CONTINUES

For the sauce: In a small, heavy saucepan, heat the oil until shimmering. Add the garlic and shallots and cook, lowering the heat when it starts sizzling. Cook, stirring with a slotted spoon, until the shallots are golden brown but not burned, just a few minutes. Scoop the garlic and shallots out of the oil with the slotted spoon and put in a food processor or blender. Add the chile flakes to the hot oil and cook until they darken a few shades—it only takes a few seconds. Remove the pan from the heat and let cool for a couple of minutes. Add the sugar, salt, and cooled oil to the processor or blender and cover the top with a folded towel. Process into a coarse purée. Scrape into a bowl and cool to room temperature. This sauce keeps for a month in the refrigerator.

For the rolls: Bring a pot of salted water to a boil for the noodles.

Cut the crab legs open with kitchen shears and remove the meat. Drain on 2 layers of paper towels. If using canned crab, pat it dry.

Stir together the fish sauce or wheat-free tamari, sugar, lemon juice, and black pepper and reserve. Set up your area for assembling the rolls as follows: a large rectangular baking dish filled with an inch of warm water, a clean kitchen towel spread out next to it, a cutting board, and a plate, damp paper towel, and plastic wrap for the finished rolls.

Once the water boils, cook the noodles according to the package instructions, stirring and testing often, until tender. Drain, rinse with cold water, and drain again. Then wrap the noodles in another kitchen towel and gently squeeze to dry thoroughly. Transfer to a bowl. Stir the reserved lemon mixture to recombine and add it to the noodles. Toss gently to coat.

To assemble the rolls, submerge a rice paper sheet in the warm water and gently swish to wet. Once the rice paper is softened but not completely limp (30 to 60 seconds, depending on the temperature of the water), carefully place it on the towel to dry and then transfer it to the cutting board. On the round, place an eighth of the crab, about ¼ cup noodles, and an eighth of the cucumber, mango, carrot, and cilantro. Fold in from the sides and roll up. Repeat with the remaining rounds and filling. Put the rolls on a plate and cover with damp paper towels and plastic wrap. Refrigerate until ready to serve.

Uncover just before serving. Serve with bowls of the chile sauce for dipping.

LASAGNA ROLLS
WITH ARRABBIATA SAUCE

Yes, lasagna can be finger food! These easy, noshy little rolls are fun for parties, whether you make them with boxed noodles or fresh pasta. They can be made a day ahead, too, and sauced at the last minute, so you can spend those last moments getting fabulous for your party.

SERVES 10

½ recipe Basic Fresh Pasta (page 29), rolled into sheets (substitute 10 boxed, dried GF lasagna noodles)

1 tablespoon extra-virgin olive oil, plus extra for pan

1 large yellow onion, minced

3 garlic cloves, chopped

1 (12 to 13-ounce) jar roasted red peppers, drained

1 teaspoon fine salt, divided

1 teaspoon red pepper flakes

1 tablespoon capers, drained

1 (15-ounce) jar artichoke hearts, drained

15 ounces ricotta cheese

½ cup shredded Parmesan cheese

½ teaspoon cracked black pepper

Bring a large pot of salted water to a boil for the pasta. Rub a sheet pan with a light coating of olive oil. Cut the pasta sheets to approximately the same size as standard lasagne noodles, by cutting each 5 x17 inch sheet in half lengthwise and crosswise, making 4 portions. You will need 10 noodles: save any leftovers for another use. Cook the fresh pasta for 2 minutes in the boiling water and then drain and pat dry. Place on the oiled sheet pan to cool. If using dried lasagna noodles, cook the pasta to al dente according to the package instructions, checking the pasta 2 to 3 minutes earlier than the recommended cooking time. Drain and place on an oiled sheet pan to cool. Rub a little oil on top of the pasta, too.

In a large sauté pan, heat the olive oil and add the onions and garlic. Sauté over medium-high heat, stirring, until they start to soften, about 5 minutes. Then lower the heat to medium-low and cook until golden and soft, about 10 minutes. Transfer half of the onion to a food processor and put the other half in a medium bowl.

To the food processor, add the drained red peppers, ½ teaspoon salt, and red pepper flakes. Process until puréed and smooth. Scrape down the bowl if necessary and repeat. Add the capers and pulse to mix. Transfer the pepper purée to a small bowl.

Drain the artichokes and finely chop half of them. Reserve the remaining for garnish.

Combine the chopped artichokes, ricotta, Parmesan, ½ teaspoon salt, and pepper with the onion in the bowl and mix well.

Divide the artichoke-ricotta filling between the lasagna sheets. Spread it down the center of the pasta, leaving a few inches at one end bare. Roll up the pasta, starting at the end with filling. Place on a plate and put long toothpicks in each roll. The rolls can be prepared to this point, covered tightly, and refrigerated for up to 24 hours.

To serve, pour the puréed pepper sauce over the rolls, arrange the remaining artichoke hearts around them, and serve at room temperature.

ROASTED RED PEPPER
AND ZUCCHINI INVOLTINI

While the average appetizer table is loaded down with bread-based nibbles such as bruschetta, yours is different. This appetizer is a great example, made up of intensely flavored sweet peppers, silky roasted zucchini, savory prosciutto, and creamy chèvre—all in cute little two-bite packages. Leave out the prosciutto if vegetarians are coming.

SERVES 6 TO 8

4 large red bell peppers

Olive oil

3 medium zucchini

8 ounces chèvre

½ cup shredded Parmesan cheese

2 cups packed fresh basil leaves, minced

8 slices prosciutto, each halved

Fine salt and freshly ground black pepper

2 tablespoons good balsamic vinegar, for drizzling

Heat the broiler on high. Roast the peppers on a sheet pan for about 6 minutes per side, or until blackened all over. Put the hot peppers in a casserole dish with a tight-fitting lid, cover, and let steam for 15 minutes. Uncover and let cool to room temperature. Then peel off and discard the charred skin and seed the peppers. Cut each into halves, then in quarters.

Preheat the oven to 400°F. Line 2 baking sheets with parchment paper or silicone baking mats and coat with olive oil. Use a mandoline or knife to slice the zucchini into ¼- to ⅓-inch-thick slices lengthwise (you want 16 slices total). Distribute the zucchini on the pans, then brush them with oil. Bake until softened but not browned, about 5 to 10 minutes. Remove from the oven and let cool to room temperature.

Mix the chèvre and Parmesan and stir in the minced basil. On each zucchini slice, place a red pepper piece, a half slice of prosciutto, a heaping tablespoon of cheese filling, and a sprinkling of salt and pepper. Roll up and skewer with toothpicks.

Serve cold or at room temperature in the summer, drizzled with balsamic vinegar. In winter, warm in the oven briefly at 350°F just to heat through, then drizzle with balsamic vinegar.

SHRIMP AND NOODLE– STUFFED AVOCADOS

Don't bore your guests with a first course of chips and salsa: roll out this dish and watch them ooh and aah. It's served in its own little avocado bowl, and who doesn't love avocados?

SERVES 8

1 (14-ounce) can full-fat coconut milk, chilled

1 tablespoon freshly squeezed lime juice, plus more as needed

½ teaspoon fine salt

12 ounces small shrimp, shelled and cooked

1 small shallot, chopped

2 medium radishes, chopped

2 ribs celery, chopped

2 tablespoons chopped fresh cilantro leaves, plus sprigs for garnish

1 (7-ounce) package shirataki noodles (substitute any other kind of cooked GF noodle)

4 large, ripe avocados

Freshly squeezed lime juice

Open the chilled coconut milk and scoop out 4 tablespoons of the thick cream, reserving the remaining for another use.

In a large bowl, combine the coconut cream, lime juice, and salt and stir to mix. Add the shrimp, shallot, radishes, celery, and chopped cilantro and toss to mix. Add the noodles and toss to mix again. Slice the avocados lengthwise and remove the pits. Sprinkle the cut surfaces with lime juice and scoop out some of the flesh, leaving at least ½ inch of avocado lining the shell. Chop the scooped-out flesh and add it to the noodle mixture. Mound the noodle mixture into the avocados and garnish with cilantro sprigs. Serve immediately.

SOBA SUSHI ROLLS WITH SPICY SALMON AND CUCUMBER GARNISH

If you thought that sushi was always made from rice, think again. Soba makes a nice, light stand-in for rice, with the benefits of whole grains. You will need a bamboo sushi mat, or makisu, to form even rolls. Always ask your fishmonger for sushi-grade fish if you are going to eat it raw.

SERVES 6

6 tablespoons wheat-free tamari

2 tablespoons grated fresh ginger

1 tablespoon granulated sugar

2 teaspoons canola oil

¼ teaspoon cayenne

8 ounces sushi-grade raw salmon

1 medium cucumber

14 ounces 100% buckwheat soba noodles

6 sheets nori

6 medium scallions, tops and bottoms trimmed

1 large carrot, cut into long strips

Mayonnaise (optional)

Pickled ginger, for serving

Wasabi paste, for serving

In a medium bowl, combine the tamari, ginger, and sugar, and stir to dissolve the sugar. Set aside.

Bring a large pot of salted water to boil for the noodles. Wrap a sushi-rolling mat with plastic wrap.

In a medium bowl, stir together the canola oil and cayenne. Finely chop the salmon, then add it to the oil and toss to coat. Let it marinate for a few minutes.

Peel, halve, and seed the cucumber. Cut one half into long, thin slivers. The other half will be used as garnish. To cut the cucumber garnish, place the other half cut-side down. Use a paring knife to cut across the cucumber in thin slices, not cutting all the way through and leaving the slices attached on one side. Cut 1-inch segments of this, and then fan out the slices.

Cook the soba according to the package directions. Drain well, rinse with warm water, and drain again. Dump out onto a double thickness of kitchen towels.

For each roll, place a sheet of nori on the plastic-covered rolling mat, shiny-side down. Grab a sixth of the noodles and drape them across the nori to cover it evenly, leaving ½ inch of nori exposed at the top, then arrange the noodles with your fingers as evenly as possible. Form a line of the salmon mixture ½ inch from the bottom of the soba, then place a scallion and cucumber and carrot strips above that. Spoon a line of mayonnaise next to the carrot, if using. Roll up just as you would a rice roll, starting at the end covered with filling, and sealing the nori with water. Let stand for a minute before slicing into 6 pieces.

Serve with the tamari-ginger dipping sauce, pickled ginger, and wasabi, and garnish with the cucumber fans.

CREAMY MACARONI-STUFFED TOMATOES

These colorful little gems are a perfect starter for your picnic, or a lively companion to a glass of wine. A simple purée of chèvre and buttermilk makes a rich, creamy dressing that's surprisingly low in fat and high in protein. Make sure you buy tomatoes that are ripe but still firm, so they will form a sturdy and tasty shell for the macaroni.

SERVES 8

8 (3-inch) tomatoes

1 garlic clove, pressed

½ cup packed parsley leaves, plus 8 sprigs for garnish

2 ounces chèvre

¼ cup buttermilk

½ teaspoon freshly cracked black pepper

¼ teaspoon fine salt

4 ounces GF macaroni (about 1¼ cup dry)

Bring a large pot of salted water to a boil for the pasta. Spread a kitchen towel on a cutting board or sheet pan.

Use a paring knife to cut a 2-inch opening in the stem end of each tomato, and then scoop out the pulp with a small spoon. Reserve ½ cup of pulp and chop it. Place each scooped-out tomato cut-side down on the towel.

In a food processor or by hand, mince the garlic and parsley together. Add the chèvre and process or mash until well mixed. Add the buttermilk, cracked pepper, and salt and process or stir until smooth.

Cook the pasta to al dente according to the package instructions, checking the pasta 2 to 3 minutes earlier than the recommended cooking time. Drain, rinse with cold water, and drain again.

In a medium bowl, combine the macaroni, tomato pulp, and chèvre mixture, and toss to mix.

Use a small spoon to stuff the macaroni mixture into the tomatoes, placing each on a serving platter or in a storage container as you go. Garnish with the parsley sprigs. Chill until serving. The tomatoes can be stored for up to 3 days in the refrigerator, tightly covered.

SPICY KIMCHI–SPIKED MAC AND CHEESE

On a cold winter night, what could be better than a bubbly, warm pot of mac and cheese? Well, I think the spicy, tangy addition of kimchi is way more exciting. Kimchi is the sauerkraut of Korea, but spicier and with more veggies. Baking these in ramekins makes a handy appetizer portion, or you can bake the whole batch in a skillet.

SERVES 6

2 tablespoons unsalted butter, plus more for the ramekins

3 tablespoons sweet rice flour

1½ cups skim milk

¼ teaspoon fine salt

8 ounces (about 2 cups) grated sharp Cheddar cheese, divided

2 large jalapeños, seeded and chopped

10 ounces GF macaroni (about 2½ cups)

6 tablespoons drained and chopped kimchi

Bring a large pot of salted water to a boil for the pasta.

Lightly butter six 1-cup ramekins and put them on a sheet pan. Preheat the oven to 400°F.

In a 2-quart saucepan, melt the butter and then whisk in the rice flour, making a smooth paste. Cook over medium heat until bubbly and toasty-smelling. Take off the heat and gradually whisk in the milk, then return to the heat. Cook, whisking frequently, until the sauce just starts to bubble and thicken. Take off the heat and whisk in the salt, all but ½ cup of the Cheddar, and the jalapeños. Let the sauce stand on the stove while you cook the pasta.

Cook the pasta 5 minutes less than the package directs, drain it, and then put it in a large bowl. Pour the cheese sauce over the macaroni and gently stir. Using a ⅓-cup measure, scoop some mac and cheese into each ramekin, then top each with a tablespoon of chopped kimchi. Tap each dish lightly against the sheet pan to even the tops. Sprinkle with the reserved Cheddar. Bake for 25 minutes, or until golden on top.

Alternatively, layer half of the macaroni mixture in an 11-inch oven-safe sauté pan, top the macaroni with half of the kimchi, then evenly distribute the remaining macaroni over the kimchi. Sprinkle with the remaining kimchi and the reserved Cheddar and bake, uncovered, for 25 to 30 minutes, or until bubbly and golden on top.

STEAMED SHRIMP DUMPLINGS
WITH CHILE DIPPING SAUCE

If you were a fan of dim sum before you gave up gluten, you must remember the dumplings with nostalgia. Now you can be your own dim sum factory at home and make big batches of these chewy, satisfying treats. And yes, they freeze well, so you can always have them on hand. You will need to have parchment paper on hand for steaming your dumplings.

SERVES 8 TO 12

¾ recipe Basic Fresh Pasta dough (page 29)

Arrowroot starch for handling the dough

1 tablespoon minced fresh ginger

2 scallions, minced

¼ cup drained water chestnuts

8 ounces shrimp, shelled and deveined

1 teaspoon cornstarch or arrowroot starch

½ teaspoon fine salt

1 teaspoon plus ½ cup granulated sugar, divided

1 teaspoon Shaoxing wine or sherry

1 teaspoon sesame oil

½ cup rice vinegar

1 tablespoon red pepper flakes

Wheat-free tamari, for serving

Use scissors to cut 24 (3-inch) parchment paper squares, one for each dumpling.

Divide the pasta dough into 24 ½-ounce pieces. Use arrowroot starch as needed for handling the dough. You can do this by dividing the dough into 4 pieces, then rolling each piece into a cylinder and cutting it into 6 even portions. Or you can cut portions and weigh each one. Form the pieces into flat rounds and cover with plastic wrap.

In a food processor or by hand, mince the ginger, and then add the scallion and water chestnuts and pulse or coarsely chop. Add the shrimp and pulse to chop, not purée. Scrape the mixture out into a small bowl and stir in the starch, salt, sugar, Shaoxing wine, and sesame oil.

To shape the dumplings, use a rolling pin and plenty of starch to roll out 3½-inch-long ovals. Use a pastry brush to dampen one edge of the oval. Measure out the filling, scooping up a slightly rounded teaspoon for each dumpling. Place a mound of filling in the center and pull the dough up to make a dumpling, gently pressing the bottom against the counter to flatten it and pinching the dough to seal. Pleat the top, then place each on a square of parchment and put on a steamer tray or plate.

To make the dipping sauce, combine the vinegar, sugar, and red pepper flakes in a small saucepan and bring to a boil over high heat. Take off the heat and let cool to room temperature.

To steam the dumplings, boil an inch of water in a wide pan. Place the steamer tray in the pan and cover. Cook, in batches if necessary, for 8 minutes, or until the shrimp is pink. Serve immediately with tamari and small bowls of the chile dipping sauce.

TOFU, SHIITAKE, AND WATER CHESTNUT POT STICKERS

Pot stickers are the best of both worlds: fried to a golden crunch on the bottom, then steamed to a tender bite on top. For a dramatic color, try the Buckwheat Pasta dough (page 30) for these—they will be unlike any pot stickers you have ever had. Jumbo-size pot stickers are easier to make, and very impressive to serve!

SERVES 8

1 ounce dried shiitake mushrooms

14 ounces firm tofu, wrapped in a towel and pressed with a heavy pan for 1 hour

1 tablespoon minced fresh ginger

½ cup drained water chestnuts, minced

¼ cup packed fresh basil, chopped

½ teaspoon fine salt

2 teaspoons sesame oil

4 scallions, minced

2 teaspoons arrowroot starch, plus more as needed for rolling

¾ recipe Basic Fresh Pasta (page 29) or Buckwheat Pasta (page 30)

2 tablespoons vegetable oil

½ to 1 cup vegetable stock

Wheat-free tamari, for serving

Sriracha or other hot sauce, for serving

Red wine vinegar, for serving

Bring 2 cups of water to a boil for the mushrooms.

Pour the boiling water over the mushrooms in a heat-safe cup, to cover. When softened (after about 10 minutes), drain the mushrooms and wring them dry in a kitchen towel, then mince. Crumble the tofu into a small bowl. Add the minced mushrooms, ginger, water chestnuts, basil, salt, sesame oil, scallions, and 2 teaspoons of arrowroot, and toss to combine.

Dust a sheet pan or deep roasting pan with arrowroot. Set out a small pastry brush and a cup of water.

Divide the pasta dough into 3 portions. Roll out each portion in a pasta-rolling machine up to setting #5 (see page 24) to make long, 1/16- inch-thick pieces. Use a chef's knife to slice each sheet of pasta in half lengthwise, then cut each half into 6 (3-inch) square pieces.

On a counter or cutting board, lay out several squares of dough. Place a tablespoon of the tofu filling in the center of each. Paint the top half of the dough wrap with water. Pull up the opposite top and bottom corners of the wrap, forming a triangle, and press them together, pushing out the excess air. Press the dough together in a point and gently push the dough against the countertop to make a flat bottom. Pinch and pleat the top of the seam decoratively, if you wish. Put each finished pot sticker on the arrowroot-coated pan. Cover with plastic wrap as you work to keep the finished pot stickers from drying out. Cover the pan and chill in the refrigerator until you are ready to cook.

To cook, heat a 14-inch frying pan with a tight-fitting lid or two smaller pans with tight-fitting lids over high heat. When hot, add the vegetable oil. When the oil is shimmering, drop the pot stickers in quickly, not allowing them to touch, with the flat side down. Cook undisturbed until the edges begin to brown, about 2 to 3 minutes. Check the bottoms—you want a browned and crisp bottom on each. If using one big pan, add 1/2 cup of the stock; if using two, add 1/2 cup to each pan, then lower the heat to medium and cover to keep the steam in. Cook for 4 minutes. When the wrappers are soft and translucent on top, lift out the pot stickers with a slotted spatula.

Serve hot with tamari, hot sauce, and red wine vinegar. Each diner can mix the three condiments to his or her own taste.

COLD NOODLES AND PASTA SALADS

When the weather is sultry, the last thing anyone wants is a hot, heavy meal. That's where lively fresh noodle dishes and pasta salads come in.

Slippery rice noodles, hearty soba noodles, and your favorite gluten-free pastas are perfect summer fare when combined with ultra-fresh seasonal produce. The textural contrasts between toothy pasta and crunchy veggies, accented with soft cheese or chewy meats and seafood make these cold dishes exciting enough to whet any appetite. Loads of color and flavor give them a pop that draws you in, whether on the buffet table at a picnic or simply served at the dinner table.

Asian noodles excel in cold dishes, which they have been used in for centuries. Rice vermicelli or bean thread noodles are great cold or hot. They do absorb dressing, like all noodles, so your noodle salad may be a little less juicy after a day in the refrigerator. If necessary, you can add a little more of the dressing to moisten it.

Standard pastas, on the other hand, can become a little stiff in the refrigerator overnight. That's why all these recipes rec-

ommend cooking the pasta at the last minute and serving the salad at room temperature. GF pastas are especially delicate in this way, so hold off on cooking the pasta component until the last possible moment. They are also absorbent and will soak up the dressing as they sit in the refrigerator.

You will not have to worry about leftovers, though, when you serve these cooling whole-meal salads. Your family will descend on the Lime-Chile Noodles with Thai Basil and Scallops (page 83) or the Cold Soba Noodles with Peanuts, Fresh Herbs, and Chicken (page 85) and clean the serving bowl. Avocado, Fresh Mozzarella, and Peach Pasta Salad (page 87) is a delightful surprise, with juicy peaches that add sweetness and tanginess. Indian flavors sing in the Biryani Vermicelli with Mixed Veggies (page 92), and the Eastern European Smoked Salmon Shells with Peas (page 91) is a perfect way to enjoy healthy salmon alongside your tender, comforting pasta.

It's summertime, and the pasta is easy. Dig into these quick and tasty recipes for a super summer meal.

LIME-CHILE NOODLES
WITH THAI BASIL AND SCALLOPS

This light, refreshing salad is quick to make and full of exciting tastes and textures. Hot, sour, salty, and sweet come together to give your noodles an irresistible sauce and to bring out all the sweetness of those delectable scallops.

SERVES 4 TO 6

3 garlic cloves, chopped

1 tablespoon minced fresh ginger

4 tablespoons freshly squeezed lime juice

3 tablespoons fish sauce

2 tablespoons palm sugar or packed light brown sugar

½ cup canned coconut milk, well-shaken

8 ounces bay scallops, trimmed

2 large red chiles, seeded and chopped (mild red Fresnos or hot Thai chiles)

8 ounces rice vermicelli or GF spaghetti

2 large carrots, julienned

½ cup packed fresh Thai basil, slivered

Bring a pot of salted water to a boil for the noodles. Stir together the garlic, ginger, lime juice, fish sauce, and sugar.

In a large sauté pan over medium-high heat, heat the coconut milk to a simmer and add the scallops and red chiles. Cook until the scallops just start to crack around the edges, about 4 to 5 minutes, depending on the size of the scallops, then add the garlic mixture and stir. Remove from the heat.

Add the noodles and carrots to the boiling water and cook for 2 to 3 minutes, or according to the package directions. Drain, rinse with hot water, drain very well, and place in a large serving bowl. Scrape the contents of the coconut and scallop sauce over the noodles and carrots, add the basil, and toss. Serve at room temperature or chilled.

COLD SZECHUAN NOODLES
WITH SRIRACHA AND CUCUMBERS

If you have been missing your Chinese takeout noodles, this recipe is the answer. All those white takeout cartons are full of wheat-flour noodles anyway, and this sauce is so easy to make that you can have your own gluten-free "takeout" faster than you can call the restaurant.

SERVES 4 TO 6

8 ounces GF fettuccine (substitute 1½ pounds sweet potato strands)

4 ounces sugar snap peas (about 1½ cups), trimmed

½ large cucumber, peeled, seeded, and thinly sliced

¾ cup Szechuan Sesame Sauce (page 47)

2 large scallions, slivered diagonally, for garnish

¼ cup black sesame seeds, for garnish

Sriracha sauce, for serving

Bring a large pot of salted water to a boil for the pasta.

Cook the pasta to al dente according to the package instructions, checking the pasta 2 to 3 minutes earlier than the recommended cooking time. Put the snap peas in the colander so that you will pour boiling water over them as you drain the pasta. Drain the pasta well, and rinse with cool water.

Shake off the excess water from the colander and transfer the pasta and snap peas to a large bowl. Add the cucumber and sesame sauce and toss to mix. Serve topped with scallions and black sesame seeds and drizzle with Sriracha sauce.

COLD SOBA NOODLES WITH PEANUTS, FRESH HERBS, AND CHICKEN

Pure buckwheat soba is one of the best-kept secrets of Japanese cuisine: it is revered as an artisanal tradition, not labeled as a gluten-free health food. Luckily, it is both, and this recipe is a simple and delicious way to show it off. If you can't find shiso, the peppery herb that also goes by "beefsteak" or "perilla leaf," use basil or parsley.

SERVES 4 TO 6

3 tablespoons wheat-free tamari

1 tablespoon sesame oil

1 tablespoon rice vinegar

1 tablespoon packed light brown sugar

1 cup fresh shiso leaves (substitute fresh basil or parsley leaves)

8 ounces 100% buckwheat soba noodles

4 ounces snow peas, trimmed

1 (8-ounce) boneless, skinless chicken breast, cooked and shredded

¼ cup chopped roasted peanuts

Bring a large pot of salted water to a boil for the noodles.

In a cup, stir together the tamari, sesame oil, rice vinegar, and brown sugar. Thinly slice the shiso leaves.

Cook the soba noodles according to the package directions and start checking for doneness 1 or 2 minutes early. Add the snow peas to the boiling water a few seconds before draining. Drain and rinse with cold water, then drain again.

Put the soba in a large bowl and drizzle the tamari mixture over it. Add the shiso and chicken and toss. Serve topped with chopped peanuts.

AVOCADO, FRESH MOZZARELLA, AND PEACH PASTA SALAD

On a hot summer day, find relief in this perky pasta salad, laced with creamy bits of avocado, sweet peaches, and soft fresh mozzarella. Keep it simple and seasonal, and you can't go wrong.

SERVES 6 TO 8

8 ounces GF spirals or radiatore

¼ cup freshly squeezed lemon juice

1 tablespoon freshly grated lemon zest

¼ cup extra-virgin olive oil

3 tablespoons honey or agave

½ teaspoon fine salt

1 teaspoon freshly cracked black pepper, or more to taste

1 large avocado, diced

2 large peaches, pitted and chopped

8 ounces fresh mozzarella, drained and cubed

1 cup fresh basil leaves, chopped

2 medium scallions, chopped

Bring a large pot of salted water to a boil for the pasta. Cook the pasta, checking it for doneness 3 to 4 minutes before the package directs and testing frequently.

While the pasta cooks, whisk together the lemon juice, zest, olive oil, honey or agave, salt, and pepper in a large bowl to combine. Add the avocado, peaches, mozzarella, basil, and scallion to the dressing in the bowl. Toss to mix and coat: this helps prevent the avocado from browning.

When the pasta is done, drain it, rinse with cold water, and drain again. Add to the bowl with the dressing and toss to mix. Serve at room temperature or chill before serving. Keeps for up to 24 hours in the refrigerator, tightly covered.

SUN-DRIED TOMATO PESTO FUSILLI SALAD WITH CRISPED HALLOUMI

Sun-dried tomatoes are a concentrated source of sweet, tangy tomato flavor, and a quick way to add depth and complexity to an easy sauce. Here, they coat your lovely fusilli and get plenty of backup flavor from seared cauliflower and halloumi. If you have not had halloumi cheese, it is a firm, non-melting cheese that can be seared or grilled to form a delicious golden crust. Paneer cheese, *kefalotyri*, and some young Mexican cheeses can be substituted.

SERVES 6 TO 8

½ cup sun-dried tomatoes

Boiling water, as needed

½ teaspoon red pepper flakes

2 garlic cloves, peeled

½ cup packed fresh parsley leaves

5 tablespoons extra-virgin olive oil, divided

12 ounces cauliflower, sliced into big florets with 1 or 2 flat sides to brown in the pan (about 4 cups sliced)

8 ounces GF fusilli or spirals

8 ounces halloumi cheese, cubed

Freshly cracked black pepper

Bring a large pot of salted water to a boil for the pasta. Place the sun-dried tomatoes in a heat-safe cup or bowl and cover with the boiling water. Let soak until very soft, 10 to 15 minutes, depending on how dry they are. Drain well, squeezing out the excess water into the cup. Reserve the soaking liquid.

Put the sun-dried tomatoes, red pepper flakes, garlic, and parsley in the food processor and pulse to chop. Add 3 tablespoons of the olive oil and process, scraping down as needed to get a smooth purée. Add a tablespoon or two of the reserved soaking water just to make a smooth, pourable sauce.

Drop the cauliflower pieces into the boiling water and cook for 2 to 3 minutes, then scoop out with a slotted spoon into a colander, leaving the water boiling for the pasta. Drain the cauliflower and pat dry.

Cook the pasta to al dente according to the package instructions, checking the pasta 2 to 3 minutes earlier than the recommended cooking time. Drain well and rinse with cold water, then toss with the sun-dried tomato pesto.

Heat the remaining 2 tablespoons of olive oil in a large sauté pan, and sear the cauliflower until browned on each side. Scoop out the cauliflower, put it in the bowl with the pasta, then add the cubed halloumi to the pan. Sear on one side without moving for about 3 minutes, then flip the pieces, and cook for about 3 minutes more to sear the other side. Sprinkle with cracked black pepper and scatter on top of the pasta salad. Serve.

MUSHROOM AND LEMON CAPRESE

The classic caprese is such a mainstay of summer salads that it can now be reinterpreted and tweaked into a pasta salad. Fresh white button mushrooms are a nice surprise here, still firm, and bathed in lemony vinaigrette.

SERVES 6 TO 8

8 ounces button mushrooms, wiped and halved

4 medium ripe tomatoes, sliced

8 ounces fresh mozzarella, drained and sliced

1 cup packed fresh basil leaves, torn

1 tablespoon freshly grated lemon zest

3 tablespoons freshly squeezed lemon juice

2 garlic cloves, pressed

4 tablespoons extra-virgin olive oil

1 teaspoon red pepper flakes

½ teaspoon fine salt, plus more as needed

8 ounces GF fusilli, spirals, or penne

Bring a large pot of salted water to a boil for the pasta. In a large bowl, combine the mushrooms, tomatoes, mozzarella, and basil. In a cup, whisk the lemon zest, juice, garlic, olive oil, red pepper flakes, and salt.

Cook the pasta to al dente according to the package instructions, checking the pasta 2 to 3 minutes earlier than the recommended cooking time. Drain, rinse with cold water and drain well. Add to the bowl with the mushrooms, then pour the lemon mixture over the pasta. Toss to coat and serve at room temperature.

This salad keeps for a day or two in the refrigerator, tightly covered.

GREEK PASTA SALAD WITH FETA, GRAPE TOMATOES, AND SPINACH

Spinach and feta seem to be a combination that appeals to everyone, especially with pasta. Look for a softer feta, like sheep's or goat's milk feta, instead of the harder, saltier style. Rinse brine-soaked feta lightly to remove some of the excess salt, and the flavor of the milk can shine through.

SERVES 4 TO 6

4 cups fresh baby spinach, coarsely chopped

4 ounces feta cheese, crumbled

1½ cups grape tomatoes, halved

2 cloves garlic, pressed

2 tablespoons red wine vinegar

¼ cup extra-virgin olive oil

½ teaspoon fine salt

1 teaspoon red pepper flakes

1 teaspoon dried oregano

8 ounces GF penne or macaroni

Bring a pot of salted water to a boil for the pasta. In a large bowl, combine the spinach, cheese, and grape tomatoes. In a cup or bowl, whisk the vinegar, olive oil, garlic, salt, red pepper flakes, and oregano. Cook the pasta according to the package directions, checking 2 to 3 minutes earlier than the recommended cooking time to be sure you don't over-cook it.

Drain the pasta and rinse with hot water, tossing gently to drain. Add the warm pasta to the bowl with the spinach and toss—the spinach should wilt a bit from the heat of the pasta. Drizzle the vinegar mixture over the pasta in the bowl and toss to coat. Serve at room temperature or chill for an hour or so.

EASTERN EUROPEAN SMOKED SALMON SHELLS WITH PEAS

Looking for a quick salad to take to a party? In the time it takes to cook the pasta, you can stir up the dressing, chop the cucumber, and slice the salmon, then just toss it all together and go. This would be good with pasta spirals, too.

SERVES 4 TO 6

8 ounces medium GF shells or penne

½ cup sour cream

1 tablespoon freshly squeezed lemon juice

2 teaspoons dried dill

½ teaspoon fine salt

1 teaspoon red pepper flakes

1 medium cucumber, peeled, seeded, and sliced

1 cup frozen peas, thawed

2 large scallions, chopped

8 ounces smoked salmon or lox, cut into bite-size pieces

Bring a large pot of salted water to a boil for the pasta. Add the pasta and cook to al dente according to the package directions, checking for doneness 3 to 4 minutes earlier than the recommended cooking time.

While the pasta cooks, mix the sour cream, lemon, dill, salt, and pepper flakes in a large bowl. Add the cucumbers, peas, scallions, and salmon. Drain the pasta when it is cooked through, then rinse with cold water. Drain well, add it to the bowl, and toss to mix. Serve at room temperature or chilled. Keeps, tightly covered, in the refrigerator for up to 2 days.

BIRYANI VERMICELLI
WITH MIXED VEGGIES

In this cool salad, the bright yellow turmeric paints the noodles an appealing, sunny color, and carrots and peas provide some contrast. It tastes great, too, and is a perfect side for tandoori chicken or curried kebabs on the grill.

SERVES 6 TO 8

2 tablespoons ghee or canola oil

1 small yellow onion, chopped

1 tablespoon chopped fresh ginger

1 teaspoon ground cumin

1 teaspoon turmeric

¼ teaspoon cayenne, or more to taste

2 tablespoons packed light brown sugar

1 teaspoon fine salt

½ cup raisins

3 tablespoons freshly squeezed lemon juice

8 ounces rice vermicelli or 6 ounces cellophane noodles (bean threads)

2 cups cauliflower florets

1 large carrot, chopped

1 cup frozen peas, thawed

¼ cup packed fresh cilantro leaves, for garnish

Bring a large pot of salted water to a boil for the noodles.

In a large sauté pan, heat the ghee or oil. Add the onion and sauté until translucent and soft. Add the ginger, cumin, turmeric, and cayenne and stir until fragrant. Remove the pan from the heat and add the brown sugar, salt, raisins, and lemon and mix to dissolve the sugar.

Cook the noodles according to the package directions, adding the cauliflower and carrot to the boiling water at the same time as the noodles. Drain well. Transfer the noodles, cauliflower, and carrot to the sauté pan, add the peas, and gently mix. Serve sprinkled with cilantro.

CELLOPHANE NOODLES IN MANGO-TAMARIND DRESSING

Tamarind, the exotic pod of the tamarind tree, is now readily available as an easy-to-use purée. Look for it in well-stocked groceries. It's worth seeking out, as it has a unique flavor: tart and raisiny at the same time. In this dish, puréed with sweet mango, it creates a low-fat dressing that tastes so good you won't miss the extra oil.

SERVES 6 TO 8

1 medium red Fresno chile, seeded

2 garlic cloves

1 small ripe mango, peeled and chopped, divided

1 tablespoon honey

1 tablespoon tamarind paste

1 tablespoon canola oil

1 teaspoon fine salt

1 pound boneless, skinless chicken breasts, cooked and shredded

8 ounces cherry tomatoes, halved

1 medium cucumber, peeled, seeded, and sliced

6 ounces cellophane noodles (bean threads) or 8 ounces GF spaghetti

Bring a pot of salted water to a boil for the noodles.

In a blender or food processor, process the red chile and garlic to mince. Add half of the mango, scraping down as necessary, and purée. When the mango is smoothly puréed, add the honey, tamarind, oil, and salt. Process to make a smooth dressing.

In a large bowl, combine the chicken, tomatoes, remaining mango, and cucumber. Cook the noodles according to the package directions and rinse with cold water. Drain well. Add the noodles to the bowl, drizzle with the dressing, and toss to mix. Serve at room temperature, or chill for up to a day, tightly covered.

KOREAN KIMCHI NOODLE SALAD WITH TOFU

Kimchi, the fermented cabbage salad of Korea, has become so popular in this country that it's easy to find. It's like a spicy, more interesting sauerkraut, brimming with fermented tanginess and heat. It's so flavorful that it provides instant depth to this easy salad.

SERVES 4 TO 6

1 cup kimchi

12 ounces extra-firm tofu, drained and cubed

¼ cup wheat-free tamari

2 tablespoons sesame oil

2 tablespoons granulated sugar

2 tablespoons Sriracha sauce

6 ounces flat rice noodles

2 large carrots, julienned

1 small cucumber, peeled, seeded, and sliced

4 ounces sugar snap peas (about 1½ cups), trimmed

2 large red Fresno chiles, seeded and chopped, or more to taste

Bring a large pot of salted water to a boil for the noodles.

Drain the kimchi, reserving the brine, and chop it well. Drizzle a tablespoon or so of the reserved kimchi brine on the tofu and let it marinate while you prepare the salad.

In a large bowl, whisk together the tamari, sesame oil, sugar, and Sriracha.

Cook the noodles according to the package directions, adding the carrots for the last minute to blanch to crisp-tender. Drain and rinse well. Add the noodles and carrots to the bowl with the tamari dressing, along with the kimchi, tofu, cucumber, snap peas, and red chiles. Toss gently and chill until time to serve up to 2 days.

SPICY ALMOND COLLARD GREEN "NOODLES" with CUCUMBER

The raw-food movement has brought us many things, including dark leafy green salads like this one. Collard greens are wide and flat and easily slivered into noodles, although you could use kale in a pinch. This salad is so good that you might want to try it with zucchini strands or even spaghetti.

SERVES 4 TO 6

1 pound collard greens or zucchini cut into strands, or 1 recipe Basic Fresh Pasta (page 29), cut into spaghetti and cooked

3 tablespoons almond butter

1 tablespoon chopped fresh ginger

2 tablespoons minced garlic

2 tablespoons sesame oil

3 tablespoons wheat-free tamari

2 tablespoons rice vinegar

1 tablespoon packed light brown sugar or honey

2 teaspoons chili-garlic sauce

1 medium cucumber, peeled, seeded, and sliced, for garnish

¾ cup whole almonds, toasted and chopped, for garnish

Using a chef's knife, thinly sliver the collard greens into ¼-inch-wide or smaller "noodles." Leave the stems in if you want extra crunch. Transfer the collard greens, zucchini, or pasta to a large bowl.

In a small bowl or the food processor, purée the almond butter, ginger, garlic, sesame oil, tamari, rice vinegar, brown sugar, and chili-garlic sauce. Pour over the collard greens, zucchini, or pasta. Use your hands to toss the greens and sauce, massaging and squeezing the slivers as you go. They will tenderize as you rub and soften more as the salad sits. Chill in the refrigerator for up to 2 days.

Serve topped with cucumber and chopped almonds.

MAYAN CHIPOTLE SHRIMP
AND CORN WITH SHELLS

We don't know all that much about ancient Mayan foods, except that the Mayans probably invented the smoked jalapeño chile that we know as the chipotle. For that stroke of smoky brilliance, I give them credit— even though they didn't have sour cream until well after Columbus sailed.

SERVES 4 TO 6

8 ounces medium GF shells

1 tablespoon extra-virgin olive oil

1 large yellow onion, chopped

2 garlic cloves, chopped

2 large red Fresno chiles, seeded and chopped (optional)

8 ounces shrimp, peeled and deveined

1 cup fresh corn kernels, cut from about 1 large ear

2 tablespoons fresh oregano

2 medium canned chipotle chiles in adobo sauce, chopped

¼ cup sour cream

½ teaspoon fine salt

Bring a large pot of salted water to a boil for the pasta. Cook the pasta to al dente according to package instructions, checking it 2 to 3 minutes earlier than the recommended cooking time. Drain, rinse with cool water, then drain well.

In a large sauté pan, heat the olive oil, then add the onions, garlic, and Fresno chiles, if using. Sauté, stirring, over medium heat, until the onions are golden, about 5 to 7 minutes. Add the shrimp and cook until pink, about 4 minutes. Stir in the corn, oregano, and chipotles and stir until heated through. Add the pasta, sour cream, and salt to the pan and toss to coat. Serve at room temperature or chill for up to 1 day.

GRILLED ASPARAGUS AND PEPPER PASTA SALAD

In the summertime, it is great fun to fire up the grill, especially for veggies. That bit of char and smoke makes asparagus and peppers into the stars of this simple pasta salad. Gruyère—a nutty, semi-firm Swiss-like cheese—is used here, but you can try other aged cheeses that you like, too.

SERVES 4 TO 6

1 pound asparagus, tough ends removed

1 medium red bell pepper, sliced ½ inch thick

¼ cup plus 2 teaspoons extra-virgin olive oil

Canola oil, as needed for the grill

8 ounces GF radiatore or fusilli

½ cup packed fresh basil leaves

2 tablespoons Champagne vinegar

2 tablespoons Dijon mustard

½ teaspoon fine salt

½ teaspoon freshly cracked black pepper

2 ounces Gruyère cheese, slivered

Preheat a gas grill on high, or light the coals in a charcoal grill.

Put the asparagus and peppers in a large bowl and toss with 2 teaspoons of the olive oil. Set up to grill: Crumple a paper towel and put some canola oil in a cup. Stick the paper towel in the cup, and when you are about to put the vegetables on the grill, use tongs to hold the paper towel and swab the grate with oil. Lay the asparagus on one side of the grill and arrange the pepper slices on the other side. Close the grill for 1 minute. Open and roll the asparagus to turn; as they brown and curl slightly, they are done. Return them to the bowl. Use the tongs to turn the pepper slices; they will take a few minutes longer than the asparagus. When they are marked and soft, transfer to the bowl. Let the vegetables cool completely.

Bring a large pot of salted water to a boil for the pasta. Cook the pasta to al dente according to the package instructions, checking the pasta 2 to 3 minutes earlier than the recommended cooking time. Drain, rinse with cool water, then drain well.

Chop the basil and add to the cooled vegetables.

In a cup, whisk together the vinegar, Dijon, remaining olive oil, salt, and pepper. Toss the dressing with the veggies, pasta, and Gruyère. Serve immediately.

PENNE with SLICED STEAK and PUMPKIN SEED SAUCE

It's fun to mix a cool pasta with a hot topping; in this case, seared steak is sliced and placed on the herbed, pumpkin seed–coated pasta, creating a beautiful color and flavor contrast. Sear the steak just before serving and give it a little resting time before slicing it so it will not lose all its juices.

SERVES 4 TO 6

¾ cup raw shelled pumpkin seeds (pepitas)

2 garlic cloves, peeled

1 medium jalapeño, seeded

½ cup packed fresh cilantro leaves

1 tablespoon freshly squeezed lime juice

½ cup plain yogurt

½ teaspoon fine salt, plus more as needed

8 ounces GF penne or spirals

2 large tomatoes, chopped

Freshly cracked black pepper

1 pound boneless steak, such as New York strip or top sirloin, about 1 inch thick

Canola oil

Bring a pot of salted water to a boil for the pasta.

Place the pumpkin seeds in a large skillet set over medium-high heat. Swirl the seeds in the pan to dry-toast them, until they are lightly browned and fragrant and some have popped, about 3 minutes. Immediately transfer the seeds to a bowl to cool.

Measure ½ cup of the seeds, reserving the remaining, and put them in a food processor with the garlic, jalapeño, and cilantro and process to a purée. Add the lime juice, yogurt, and salt and process until smooth and creamy.

Cook the penne to al dente according to the package directions, testing the pasta 3 minutes before the recommended cooking time. Drain and rinse the pasta in cool water, then toss with the pumpkin seed sauce. Top with chopped tomatoes.

Heat a cast-iron skillet over high heat for 3 minutes. Salt and pepper the steak generously on both sides. Drizzle a little canola oil in the pan. Sear the steak for 2 minutes per side for medium-rare. Transfer the hot steak to a cutting board and let stand for 5 minutes.

Thinly slice the steak and serve the pasta with sliced steak and the reserved pumpkin seeds on top.

PASTA SALAD WITH CHICKEN AND CHERRY TOMATOES

If you've got some leftover chicken and a box of spiral pasta, you are halfway to dinner with this simple salad. It's a little lighter, employing Greek yogurt to fill out the dressing, with just a bit of mayo for flavor.

SERVES 4 TO 6

12 ounces cooked boneless, skinless chicken breast, chopped

3 ribs celery, plus leaves, chopped

2 large scallions, chopped

1 cup halved cherry tomatoes,

½ cup packed fresh parsley leaves, chopped

½ cup plain Greek yogurt

3 tablespoons mayonnaise

½ teaspoon celery seeds

½ teaspoon fine salt

8 ounces GF spirals or medium shells

Bring a large pot of salted water to a boil for the pasta.

In a large bowl, combine the chicken, celery, scallions, cherry tomatoes, and parsley. In a medium bowl, stir together the yogurt, mayo, celery seeds, and salt.

Cook the pasta to al dente according to the package instructions, checking it 2 to 3 minutes earlier than the recommended cooking time. Drain, rinse with cold water, and drain again. Add to the chicken mixture and pour the dressing over the salad, tossing gently to mix. Chill until serving for up to 2 days.

HOT NOODLES AND PASTA

We love pasta and noodles because they are tasty and comforting. We also love them because they can be so fast and convenient. Who hasn't walked in the door after a long day at work and thrown together a pot of spaghetti or an instant noodle dish in a matter of minutes? Remember, it was the portability and utility of dried pasta that helped it spread from its countries of origin to the far corners of the globe. Being fast and easy has made dried pasta very popular.

Pasta can still be your go-to pantry meal, with today's vastly improved gluten-free dried pastas. Stock up on GF pasta and Asian noodles, and keep some staple ingredients on hand for your favorite dish. Wheat-free tamari, good jarred pasta sauces, and a few fresh veggies can be the start of a fabulous meal. Shredded cheeses freeze well, as do the sauces in the Sauces chapter, so you can have them on hand for dinner emergencies. Jars of tomatoes, roasted peppers, artichoke hearts, anchovies, capers, and olives can sit patiently in your cupboard, waiting for the day you need to make a quick meal.

So put a pot of water on to boil and get cooking.

Remember, in these recipes, with a few exceptions, you will be cooking your pasta or noodles completely. Boil them on a full boil and salt the water for most pastas. Always set your timer a few minutes earlier than the cooking time given on the package, and always test often. Try different brands to see which ones you prefer.

Browse this chapter and see which pasta dishes appeal to you. They run the gamut from quick and homey to quick and exotic, and if you are up for it, you can try making fresh pasta, gnocchi, or egg crêpe "noodles" for an extra-special meal. Pad Thai? Spaghetti with clam sauce? Bolognese, or perhaps beef and broccoli noodles? It's all here, safely gluten-free and filled with flavor.

"INSTANT" GRUYÈRE AND VEGGIE SPIRALS

It's one-pot magic, thanks to a trick I got from the back of a package of Jovial brand gluten-free pasta. Pasta and veggies simmer in a mixture of milk and water, cooking while also creating a creamy sauce. You really can have this on the table in 20 minutes, if you keep shredded cheese handy.

SERVES 2 TO 4

1½ cups milk

1½ cups water

2 tablespoons chopped yellow onion

1 medium carrot, chopped

½ teaspoon fine salt

8 ounces GF fusilli, spirals, or macaroni

½ cup frozen peas, thawed

¼ cup packed fresh parsley leaves, chopped

4 ounces Gruyère cheese, shredded

In a 4-quart saucepan, combine the milk, water, onion, carrot, and salt and bring to a boil over medium-high heat. Stir in the fusilli, return to a boil, and reduce the heat to keep it at a simmer. Stir frequently for 10 minutes.

At 10 minutes, test the pasta. The liquids should be absorbed and you should be stirring constantly to keep it from sticking. When the pasta is al dente, stir in the peas and the parsley. When they are warmed through, stir in the cheese and keep stirring until it is melted and the sauce is creamy. Serve hot.

SPAGHETTI WITH BROCCOLI, CHILES, AND CHÈVRE

This simple pasta dish is just minutes away, with an easy sauté and a quick toss with creamy chèvre cheese. A little lemon zest elevates it to extra-special, with that sparkle cutting the rich cheese and bringing out the sweetness of the broccoli.

SERVES 4 TO 6

¾ recipe Basic Fresh Pasta (page 29), cut into spaghetti, or 6 ounces GF dried spaghetti

2 tablespoons extra-virgin olive oil

2 garlic cloves, chopped

½ teaspoon red pepper flakes

4 scallions, chopped

8 ounces broccoli, cut into large florets

1 tablespoon freshly grated lemon zest

½ teaspoon fine salt

¼ cup dry white wine

2 cups packed arugula, chopped

3 ounces chèvre cheese, crumbled

Bring a large pot of salted water to a boil for the pasta. Cook the fresh pasta for about 2 minutes, or until al dente, and drain. If using dried pasta, cook to al dente, checking for doneness 3 minutes before the package directs.

In a large sauté pan, heat the olive oil over medium-high heat. Sauté the garlic and red pepper flakes for a minute, then add the scallions, broccoli, lemon zest, and salt and stir. Add the white wine and bring to a boil, then cover the pan for 2 minutes to steam the broccoli. Uncover and boil until the wine is reduced to a syrupy glaze, about 2 minutes, stirring occasionally. Stir in the arugula to wilt.

Toss the pasta with the broccoli in the pan, then fold in the chèvre. Serve hot.

PRIMAVERA PASTA

Primavera **means "spring" in Italian, and the pasta should be a celebration of spring vegetables. Here, a cornucopia of colorful spring veggies is cooked to crisp-tender and tossed with pasta, cream, and chervil. Chervil is a delicate spring herb with a subtle, parsley-like flavor. The chervil plant can't stand the intense summer heat, so it comes and goes quickly, but you can substitute parsley and enjoy this pasta anytime you'd like.**

SERVES 4 TO 5

8 ounces dried GF linguine or 1 recipe Basic Fresh Pasta (page 29), cut into linguine

2 tablespoons extra-virgin olive oil

5 small young carrots (about 5 ounces), halved

3 ounces broccoli, cut into florets

6 spears asparagus, tough bases trimmed and cut into 1-inch pieces

2 Roma tomatoes, cored, seeded, and chopped

4 ounces sugar snap peas (about 1½ cups), trimmed

1½ teaspoons freshly grated lemon zest

2 garlic cloves, minced, more or less to taste

½ cup heavy cream

½ cup packed fresh chervil leaves, chopped

Fine salt and freshly ground black pepper

¾ cup grated Parmesan cheese

Bring a large pot of salted water to a boil for the pasta.

If using dried pasta, cook while making the vegetable sauce; if using fresh, wait to cook it, since it only takes 2 minutes. Cook the dried pasta to al dente according to the package instructions, checking the pasta 2 to 3 minutes earlier than the recommended cooking time.

Heat the oil in a large nonstick sauté pan about 5 minutes before the pasta will be done. Sauté the carrots, broccoli, asparagus, tomatoes, peas, and lemon zest over medium-high heat. After about 1 minute, add the garlic and sauté briefly. Add the cream and bring to a boil to reduce, about 1 to 2 minutes. Turn off the heat, stir in the chervil, and add salt and pepper to taste.

Drain the pasta and toss with the vegetables in the pan. Add the Parmesan and toss again. Serve immediately.

PENNE IN ARTICHOKE PESTO WITH CARROTS AND BROCCOLI

Artichoke lovers will love this pasta, which is bathed in artichoke purée and accented with chopped artichokes. Look for canned or jarred artichoke bottoms, which have none of the coarse leaves or tips of artichoke hearts.

SERVES 6 TO 8

2 cups packed fresh basil leaves

2 garlic cloves

¼ cup pine nuts

¼ cup extra-virgin olive oil

1 teaspoon fine salt

12 ounces artichoke hearts or bottoms, drained, divided

8 ounces GF penne or spirals

10 ounces broccoli, cut into florets (about 4 cups)

1 small carrot, julienned

Bring a large pot of salted water to a boil for the pasta.

Put the basil, garlic, and pine nuts in a food processor and process to mince. Scrape down and process until smooth, then add the olive oil and salt and process to get a smooth pesto. Add 2 of the artichokes and process to a coarse purée. Chop the remaining artichokes and reserve.

Cook the pasta according to the package directions, checking for doneness 3 to 4 minutes before the recommended cooking time. Add the reserved artichokes, broccoli, and carrot for the last minute of cooking. Drain well.

Return the hot pasta and vegetables to the pan and add the artichoke pesto. Toss to mix. Serve hot.

PASTA WITH SPICY EGGPLANT SAUCE AND HAZELNUTS

In the Piedmont region of Italy, hazelnuts are a prized crop, making their way into Piedmont's prized Gianduja chocolates, as well as into pastas like this one. Eggplant, roasted to creamy perfection, makes an enigmatic pasta sauce and, with a sprinkling of toasted hazelnuts may well convert even the eggplant averse.

SERVES 4 TO 5

1 pound eggplant (1 large globe or 2 long Asian eggplants)

2 garlic cloves

½ cup toasted hazelnuts, skins rubbed off

4 tablespoons extra-virgin olive oil

1 teaspoon fine salt

8 ounces GF fettuccine (substitute 2 pounds spaghetti squash for veggie noodles)

½ cup packed fresh basil leaves, chopped

1 pinch red pepper flakes

Roast the eggplant first—even up to a day ahead. Preheat the oven to 400°F. Pierce the eggplant a few times with a paring knife and put it on a sheet pan. For small eggplants, roast for 40 minutes; for large eggplants, roast at least an hour, or until limp and collapsing. When cool enough to handle, slit the skins and scoop out the flesh.

Bring a large pot of salted water to a boil for the pasta.

In a food processor or blender, purée the garlic, then add the hazelnuts and pulse to chop finely. Add the eggplant to the mixture and process, streaming in the olive oil. Add the salt and blend.

Cook the pasta to al dente according to the package instructions, checking the pasta 2 to 3 minutes earlier than the recommended cooking time. Drain well.

In the pot you cooked the pasta in, heat the eggplant sauce over low heat, stirring occasionally. Add the basil and pepper flakes and toss the pasta in the sauce. Serve hot.

CREAMY CARBONARA LINGUINE

Carbonara is one of those recipes that intimidates home cooks, perhaps because it involves raw eggs. With a few tricks and pasteurized eggs, you can put your concerns to rest. Using a warm bowl to do the final mixing helps the eggs cook while coating the pasta and prevents scrambling.

SERVES 2 TO 4

2 large pasteurized eggs

½ cup grated Parmesan cheese

4 slices bacon, chopped

¼ cup dry white wine

1 clove garlic, chopped

8 ounces dried GF linguine or spaghetti

Fine salt and freshly ground black pepper

Bring a large pot of salted water to a boil for the pasta. Preheat the oven to 200°F. Put a large heat-safe bowl in the oven for mixing the pasta.

In a medium bowl, whisk the eggs and Parmesan together.

In a large sauté pan, cook the bacon over medium-high heat, reducing to medium after the bacon starts to brown. Stir and turn the bacon until it is all browned but not too crisp, about 4 minutes. Drain on paper towels. Measure a tablespoon of bacon fat and whisk it into the egg mixture, then pour off and discard the remaining fat. Add the wine and garlic to the pan and bring to a boil to deglaze the pan, about 2 minutes. Return the cooked bacon to the pan and keep warm.

Cook the pasta to al dente according to the package instructions, checking the it 2 to 3 minutes earlier than the recommended cooking time. When draining the pasta, reserve ¼ cup of the pasta water and stir it into the bacon in the pan. Immediately (and carefully) take the hot bowl out of the oven, dump the pasta in it, and scrape in the bacon mixture. Pour in the whisked egg mixture while stirring. Stir until the pasta is fully coated, the cheese melts, and the eggy sauce thickens. Taste and season with salt and pepper.

Serve immediately.

FUSILLI WITH PORK TENDERLOIN AND APPLES

Pork and apples are often paired, whether in a pork chop and applesauce dinner or a roast pork with sliced apples. In this quick sauté, slices of lean tenderloin are browned with sage and apples, then the pan is deglazed with cream and Marsala for a flavorful sauce. Tangy Gorgonzola provides an accent at the end.

SERVES 4 TO 6

8 ounces GF fusilli, spirals, or spaghetti

8 ounces pork tenderloin

1 teaspoon olive oil

1 tablespoon minced fresh sage

2 medium sweet apples, peeled, cored, and sliced

2 garlic cloves, minced

½ cup heavy cream

¼ cup Marsala wine

½ teaspoon fine salt

½ teaspoon freshly ground black pepper

4 tablespoons crumbled Gorgonzola cheese, for garnish

Bring a large pot of salted water to a boil for the pasta. Cook the pasta to al dente according to the package instructions, checking it 2 to 3 minutes earlier than the recommended cooking time. Drain well.

Slice the pork across the grain into thin medallions.

In a large sauté pan, heat the oil over medium-high heat. Add the pork in batches and sear on one side for at least a minute or two before turning and searing the other side. Sear but don't overcook. Transfer the pork to a plate while you cook the rest. When the last batch of pork has been seared and transferred to the plate, add the sage, apples, garlic, cream, wine, salt, and pepper to the pan.

Cook about 1 minute over medium-high heat to reduce the liquid by half. Return the pork to the pan. Add the pasta and toss to coat with the sauce. Serve sprinkled with Gorgonzola.

SPICY FUSILLI AND ESCAROLE WITH YELLOW SQUASH

If you have not yet discovered escarole, allow me to introduce you to this delicious, slightly bitter green. Here, it provides a spicy note and melts into the veggie medley with the pasta. If you can't find escarole, look for broccoli raab, or in a pinch, Tuscan kale.

SERVES 4 TO 6

1 tablespoon extra-virgin olive oil

2 cups cherry tomatoes, halved

8 ounces escarole (one small head), chopped

2 small yellow squash, julienned

2 large jalapeños, seeded and chopped

3 garlic cloves, chopped

1 tablespoon freshly grated lemon zest

½ teaspoon fine salt

½ teaspoon freshly cracked black pepper

8 ounces GF fusilli, spirals, or penne

½ cup shredded Asiago cheese, for garnish

Bring a large pot of salted water to a boil for the pasta.

Prepare the vegetables and keep them all in separate piles. In a large sauté pan, heat the olive oil and add the cherry tomatoes. Sauté over medium-high heat until the tomatoes start to pop and soften. Add the escarole and squash and stir until the greens start to wilt and the squash starts to brown. Add the jalapeños, garlic, and lemon zest and stir until fragrant. Add the salt and pepper and taste for seasoning.

Cook the pasta to al dente according to the package instructions, checking it 2 to 3 minutes earlier than the recommended cooking time. Toss it in the pan with the vegetables and sprinkle with Asiago cheese. Serve hot.

GREEN OLIVE AND SERRANO PESTO FUSILLI WITH ROASTED CAULIFLOWER

Pesto has become as American as pizza and spaghetti and meatballs, so it's only fitting that we interpret it in all sorts of ways. In this tasty version, hot serranos give the basil a lively kick. If you are sensitive to spice, you can substitute milder jalapeños to taste.

SERVES 4 TO 6

8 ounces cauliflower, cut into florets (about 3 heaping cups)

1 large carrot, julienned

½ cup chopped red onion

2 tablespoons capers, rinsed and drained

3 cups packed fresh basil leaves

2 garlic cloves, peeled

2 medium serrano chiles, seeded

4 large green olives, pitted

½ teaspoon fine salt

¼ cup extra-virgin olive oil, plus more as needed

½ recipe Basic Fresh Pasta (page 29), cut into linguine, or 1 pound dried GF linguine

Bring a large pot of salted water to a boil for the pasta.

Preheat the oven to 400°F. Toss the cauliflower, carrot and red onion with a drizzle of olive oil on a rimmed sheet pan and roast for 20 minutes. The cauliflower should be golden in spots and tender. Sprinkle the capers over the hot vegetables.

Combine the basil, garlic, serranos, and olives in a food processor. Pulse until minced. Add the salt and then the ¼ cup olive oil in a steady stream and process to a smooth paste.

Cook the fresh pasta for about 2 minutes, or cook the dried pasta to al dente according to the package instructions, checking the pasta 2 to 3 minutes earlier than the recommended cooking time. Drain well and return the pasta to the pot. Add the cauliflower and carrot mixture to the pasta. Add the pesto and toss to coat, stirring over low heat just to warm, if necessary. Serve immediately.

GNOCCHI IN SALMON–ANCHOVY SAUCE WITH CURRANTS

Pillowy gnocchi are such a comforting treat. In this simple dish, a quick sauté and some good-quality canned fish make a meal from your homemade gnocchi. It's a perfect way to enjoy the fruits of your labor.

SERVES 4 TO 6

¼ cup extra-virgin olive oil, plus more as needed

2 teaspoons freshly grated lemon zest

3 garlic cloves, chopped

1½ ounces canned whole anchovies, drained

1 to 2 teaspoons red pepper flakes

1 recipe Potato Gnocchi (page 31)

1 cup packed fresh parsley leaves, chopped

1 (8-ounce) can water-packed salmon, drained

¼ cup dried currants

Bring a large pot of salted water to a boil for the gnocchi.

In a large sauté pan, heat the olive oil briefly, then add the lemon zest, garlic, anchovies, and red pepper flakes. Stir, breaking up the anchovies as you go. Cook just until heated through, about 2 minutes.

Drop the gnocchi 12 at a time into the boiling water. As the gnocchi float to the surface, remove them with a slotted spoon to a colander. Drizzle with oil and toss gently to keep them from sticking together. Add the gnocchi to the sauté pan along with the parsley, salmon, and currants. Stir to coat and warm through. Serve hot.

GNOCCHI WITH ROASTED TOMATO–OLIVE SAUCE

In the wintertime, grape tomatoes, sometimes called Santa Sweets, are the best-tasting fresh tomatoes in the market. I love to roast them to concentrate the sweetness and make a chunky sauce for these pillowy gnocchi.

SERVES 4 TO 6

3 cups grape tomatoes

2 tablespoons extra-virgin olive oil, divided, plus more as needed

1 large yellow onion, chopped

2 garlic cloves, minced

½ cup dry white wine

¼ teaspoon red pepper flakes

1 tablespoon sun-dried tomato paste

1 cup pitted kalamata olives

Fine salt and freshly ground black pepper

1 recipe Potato Gnocchi (page 31)

Parmesan cheese, for serving

Preheat the oven to 400°F. Toss the tomatoes with 1 tablespoon of olive oil to coat and roast on a rimmed sheet pan for 1 hour, stirring every 20 minutes, until very soft and collapsed in their skins.

Bring a large pot of salted water to a boil for the gnocchi.

In a large sauté pan, heat 1 tablespoon olive oil and sauté the onions and garlic until softened. Add the wine, pepper flakes, tomato paste, and olives and simmer until thick, about 5 minutes. Season to taste with salt and pepper.

Drop the gnocchi 12 at a time into the boiling water. As the gnocchi float to the surface, remove them with a slotted spoon to a colander. Drizzle with oil and toss gently to keep them from sticking together. Add the gnocchi to the sauce and toss, or put the gnocchi on a platter and pour the sauce over them. Pass Parmesan to grate at the table.

Gnocchi with Roasted
Tomato–Olive Sauce
p. 117

Spicy Brussels
Sprout and
Anchovy Spaghetti
p. 120

SPICY BRUSSELS SPROUT
AND ANCHOVY SPAGHETTI

Sweet, crunchy Brussels sprouts take on a nutty character when sautéed over high heat until well browned and softened. Add some salty, umami-rich anchovies and you have a riot of vegetable goodness to toss with pasta.

SERVES 4 TO 6

8 ounces GF spaghetti (substitute 4 cups Egg Crêpe "Noodles," page 38)

2 tablespoons extra-virgin olive oil

1 large yellow onion, chopped

2 garlic cloves, chopped

1 pound Brussels sprouts, trimmed and thinly sliced

2 teaspoons red pepper flakes

1 tablespoon anchovy paste

2 ounces Parmesan cheese, finely shredded

Bring a large pot of salted water to a boil for the pasta.

Cook the pasta to al dente according to the package instructions, checking for doneness 3 to 4 minutes before the recommended cooking time. Drain well.

In a large sauté pan, heat the olive oil over medium-high heat and sauté the onion for a few minutes to soften. Add the garlic and Brussels sprouts and cook over medium-high heat, stirring. As the Brussels sprouts soften and get some brown spots, about 5 minutes, add the red pepper flakes and anchovy paste, smashing it on the bottom of the pan and stirring it in. When the Brussels sprouts are tender and have plenty of golden brown on them, about 2 minutes more, add the spaghetti to the pan and toss to coat. Take the pan off the heat and add the Parmesan, toss to mix, and serve.

ITALIAN ASPARAGUS, RICOTTA, AND PEPPER SPIRALS

Thanks to creamy, sweet ricotta, this pasta has an instant sauce. Asparagus is one of the fastest veggies to prepare, too: just cut it into 1-inch pieces starting at the tips, and stop when you get to the tough bottoms. If you don't want too much heat, use mild wax or bell peppers.

SERVES 4 TO 6

8 ounces GF spirals or penne

2 tablespoons extra-virgin olive oil

1 large yellow onion, chopped

2 garlic cloves, chopped

½ teaspoon red pepper flakes

2 large yellow Hungarian wax chiles, seeded and thinly sliced (substitute 1 large red bell pepper for less heat)

1 pound asparagus, chopped

1 cup ricotta cheese

½ teaspoon fine salt

Bring a large pot of salted water to a boil for the pasta. Cook the pasta to al dente according to the package instructions, checking it 2 to 3 minutes earlier than the recommended cooking time. Drain well.

In a large sauté pan, heat the olive oil over medium-high heat, then sauté the onion until softened, about 5 minutes. Add the garlic, pepper flakes, chiles or peppers, and asparagus. Sauté, stirring, just until the asparagus is crisp-tender and the chiles are softened. Add the ricotta cheese and salt and stir to mix and heat the ricotta gently. Add the pasta to the pan and toss to coat. Serve hot.

SPAGHETTI IN SPICY CLAM SAUCE WITH SCALLIONS AND PARSLEY

Clam sauce is classic, simple, and bursting with the flavor of the sea. You can use either fresh clams or canned, depending on availability. If you use fresh clams, get the smallest ones you can and give your diners an empty bowl for the shells.

SERVES 4 TO 6

¼ cup extra-virgin olive oil

1 medium yellow onion, chopped

6 garlic cloves, chopped

1 teaspoon red pepper flakes

½ cup dry white wine

½ cup bottled clam juice

12 ounces GF spaghetti or linguine

2 pounds small clams, scrubbed (substitute one 10-ounce can, drained)

2 tablespoons unsalted butter

½ cup packed fresh parsley leaves, chopped

4 large scallions, chopped

In a large sauté pan, heat the olive oil over medium heat and sauté the onion for about 5 minutes, or until softened. Add the garlic and stir until fragrant, 1 minute, then add the red pepper flakes and stir 1 minute more. Add the wine and clam juice and bring to a boil. Boil for 5 minutes to reduce slightly.

Bring a large pot of salted water to a boil for the pasta. Cook the pasta to al dente according to the package instructions, checking it 2 to 3 minutes earlier than the recommended cooking time. Drain well.

While the pasta cooks, stir the clams into the sauce and simmer, covered, stirring occasionally. The clams should all open in 4 to 6 minutes. Discard any clams that have not opened. (If using canned clams, just toss in the pan to heat through, about 3 minutes.) Remove the pan from the heat and stir in the butter. Add the pasta, parsley, and scallions to the sauce and toss until well mixed. Serve in wide, flat bowls.

FRESH PASTA WITH ALMONDS, OLIVES, AND TUNA

If you go to the effort to make fresh pasta, show it off in a dish like this. The chewy, bouncy pasta is adorned with salty, chunky hunks of olive, tuna, and almond to create a mouthful of sensations. It's also a quick one to put together with dried pasta on a busy night.

SERVES 4 TO 6

3 tablespoons extra-virgin olive oil

3 garlic cloves, thinly sliced

3 medium tomatoes, cored and chopped

¼ cup pitted kalamata olives, chopped

1 recipe Basic Fresh Pasta (page 29), cut into fettuccine (substitute 8 ounces dried GF fettuccine)

¼ cup slivered almonds, toasted and chopped

¼ cup GF breadcrumbs or crushed rice cereal

½ cup packed fresh parsley leaves, chopped

2 (5-ounce) cans tuna, drained

1 teaspoon fine salt

1 teaspoon freshly cracked black pepper

Bring a pot of salted water to a boil for the pasta.

In a large sauté pan, heat the olive oil over medium heat and add the sliced garlic. Cook until the garlic sizzles and browns a little around the edges, about 2 minutes. Add the tomatoes and olives and stir, increasing the heat to medium-high. Cook just until the mixture is heated through.

Cook the fresh pasta for 2 minutes, or until al dente. If using dried pasta, cook to al dente according to the package instructions, checking for doneness 3 to 4 minutes before the recommended cooking time. Drain well.

Add the pasta, almonds, breadcrumbs, parsley, tuna, and salt and pepper to the pan and fold together gently. Heat until everything is warmed through and serve immediately.

CACIO E PEPE PASTA

Sometimes simple is best. Nothing but a sensuous anointing of butter, melting cheese, and freshly cracked black pepper makes this classic dish unforgettable. For a modern twist, try it with zucchini noodles. It's guaranteed to be the most popular veggie on the table.

SERVES 2 TO 4

¾ recipe Basic Fresh Pasta, page 29, cut into linguine (substitute 12 ounces zucchini)

3 tablespoons unsalted butter

2 teaspoons black peppercorns, coarsely crushed

1 cup finely grated aged Asiago

½ teaspoon fine salt

Bring a large pot of salted water to a boil to cook the pasta. Cook the pasta for 2 minutes, just until al dente. Drain well, rinse with hot water, and proceed. If using zucchini, use a vegetable peeler or a mandoline to cut the zucchini into long strands (you should have about 4 heaping cups).

In a large sauté pan, melt the butter. Add the cracked pepper and sauté over medium-low heat for about 5 minutes, to really infuse the butter. Add the pasta or zucchini and toss in the pan over medium-high heat, just to coat (or start to soften the zucchini, if using). Toss in the cheese and salt and turn the pasta in the pan until the cheese is melted. Serve immediately.

MALTAGLIATI with CHARD, LENTILS, and SMOKED PAPRIKA

Sometimes, messy is good. At least in the case of these haphazardly shaped pieces of pasta, which curl around and catch the hearty sauce of lentils and greens. It's also a good way to use up any broken lasagna noodles left in the bottom of the box. Waste not, want not!

SERVES 4

½ cup French green lentils

3 cups water

¼ cup extra-virgin olive oil

1 large carrot, julienned

8 ounces chard, stemmed and chopped

2 garlic cloves, chopped

2 tablespoons fresh thyme leaves, chopped

½ to 1 teaspoon smoked paprika, or to taste

1 teaspoon fine salt

1 teaspoon freshly cracked black pepper

½ recipe Basic Fresh Pasta (page 29), rolled into 4 sheets (substitute 6 ounces dried GF lasagna noodles)

Combine the lentils and the water in a small pot and bring to a boil. When the water boils, reduce the heat to simmer for about 30 minutes. Check the lentils every 5 minutes after that. They should be tender but not falling apart. Drain.

Bring a large pot of salted water to a boil for the pasta.

In a large sauté pan, heat the olive oil over medium-high heat and add the carrots. Stir for 3 minutes, just to soften a bit, then add the chard and stir for a minute to wilt. Add the garlic, thyme and smoked paprika and stir, then add the salt and pepper and cook until the chard is just tender. Reduce the heat to medium and stir in the lentils to warm them through.

Chop the fresh pasta into irregular, bite-size pieces, or break the lasagna noodles. Add to the boiling water and cook until just al dente, about 2 minutes for the fresh pasta. If using dried pasta, cook to al dente according to the package instructions, checking for doneness 3 to 4 minutes before the recommended cooking time.

Drain the pasta and add it to the chard mixture. Fold it all together and serve hot.

PENNE WITH TUSCAN KALE AND BLUE CHEESE

Now that blue cheese is off the list of banned foods for GF diners, all that flavor is yours to enjoy. Hearty Tuscan kale is perfect for this, but any kale will do. The minerally, slightly bitter taste is a perfect foil for melting crumbles of funky blue.

SERVES 4 TO 6

2 tablespoons extra-virgin olive oil

1 medium yellow onion, chopped

2 tablespoons packed fresh sage leaves, chopped

1 large carrot, julienned

3 garlic cloves, chopped

8 ounces Tuscan kale, stemmed and coarsely chopped

½ cup half-and-half

½ teaspoon fine salt

1 teaspoon freshly cracked black pepper

8 ounces GF penne or spaghetti

½ cup crumbled GF blue cheese

Bring a large pot of water to a boil for the pasta.

In a large sauté pan, heat the olive oil briefly over medium-high heat. Add the onion, sage, and carrot and cook, stirring, until softened. Reduce the heat to medium and cook for 5 to 10 minutes. When the onions are golden and soft, add the garlic and kale and stir, turning the leaves in the pan until they start to wilt. Add the half-and-half, salt, and pepper and increase the heat to medium-high to bring to a boil. Cook until the half-and-half is thick and coats the leaves.

Cook the pasta to al dente according to the package instructions, checking it 2 to 3 minutes earlier than the recommended cooking time. Toss the pasta in the pan with the kale mixture and then toss in the blue cheese. Serve hot.

PASTA CACCIATORE
WITH CHICKEN THIGHS

Cacciatore is a "hunter's pasta" and harkens back to a simple dish an Italian hunter might cook up after a day in the woods. We know it as a tomato-sauced chicken dish, spiked with anchovy and spice. This version gets extra depth from lemon zest and fresh thyme and the hearty flavor of dark meat instead of the ubiquitous breast. If possible, prepare the chicken and herbs the night before so that it can spend extra time marinating in the refrigerator.

SERVES 4 TO 6

1 pound boneless, skinless chicken thighs

2 tablespoons fresh thyme leaves, minced

2 garlic cloves, chopped

½ teaspoon fine salt

3 tablespoons extra-virgin olive oil, divided

Freshly ground black pepper

1 teaspoon freshly grated lemon zest

½ cup chopped yellow onion

½ teaspoon red pepper flakes

2 cups cherry tomatoes, halved

1 teaspoon anchovy paste

1 tablespoon salted capers, rinsed and patted dry

½ cup tomato sauce

½ cup packed fresh parsley leaves, chopped

8 ounces GF penne or spirals

½ cup shredded Parmesan cheese, for serving

Dice the chicken into small, bite-size pieces. Mince the thyme and garlic together and then make a paste with the salt, pepper to taste, and lemon zest, mashing them together. Stir the paste into 2 tablespoons of the olive oil and combine with the chicken in a bowl or a resealable plastic bag, mixing to coat thoroughly. Refrigerate, covered, for at least 2 hours and up to overnight.

Bring a large pot of salted water to a boil for the pasta.

Heat a large skillet over medium-high heat and add the remaining 1 tablespoon oil. Add the onions and red pepper flakes and scatter the chicken in the pan. Sear and brown well, stirring every few minutes, until the chicken is completely cooked, about 5 minutes. Add the cherry tomatoes, anchovy paste, and capers and stir until the tomatoes soften, about 4 minutes. Add the tomato sauce and cook, stirring, until thick, about 3 minutes. Add the parsley and stir to mix.

Cook the pasta to al dente according to the package instructions, checking for doneness 3 to 4 minutes before the recommended cooking time. Drain well.

Toss the hot pasta with the sauce to coat and serve with Parmesan on the side.

CHICKEN ARRABBIATA WITH ARTICHOKES AND PASTA

Sweet roasted red peppers make a creamy sauce for pasta: a nice change from tomato sauces. This is a good pantry pasta: keep the peppers and artichokes handy and you can put it together on a weeknight in a snap.

SERVES 4

1 (12-ounce) jar roasted red peppers

¼ cup extra-virgin olive oil

1 small red onion, chopped

2 large garlic cloves, chopped

1 teaspoon fine salt

Freshly cracked black pepper

1 teaspoon red pepper flakes (or to taste)

3 tablespoons salt-packed capers, rinsed and drained

1 pound roasted boneless, skinless chicken breasts, shredded

1 (15-ounce) jar artichoke bottoms or hearts, drained and sliced

8 ounces GF spaghetti or 16 ounces shirataki

½ cup packed fresh basil leaves, chopped, plus 4 sprigs basil, for garnish

Bring a large pot of salted water to a boil for the pasta.

Drain and rinse the peppers and pat them dry on a kitchen towel. Chop coarsely.

In a large sauté pan, heat the olive oil. Add the onion and garlic and sauté until very soft. Add the roasted red peppers, salt, black pepper, and red pepper flakes and continue cooking for about 5 minutes. Purée the mixture in a blender or food processor. Return the sauce to the stovetop to keep warm and add the capers, chicken, and artichokes, stirring to heat gently.

Cook the pasta. Add a few extra pieces of pasta and start checking for doneness 3 to 4 minutes before the package directs. Check often, and when it reaches al dente, drain immediately.

Add the pasta to the sauce and heat through, tossing to mix, then add the chopped basil. Garnish with basil sprigs and serve.

HUNGARIAN CABBAGE NOODLES
WITH KIELBASA

Peasant food often stretches a small portion of meat with copious amounts of inexpensive vegetables, such as cabbage. Now we can enjoy that method for its healthfulness and flavor as well as its economy. Spicy kielbasa infuses a red glow into the tangy wine sauce and seasons the whole dish.

SERVES 4 TO 6

1 tablespoon extra-virgin olive oil

4 cups chopped cabbage (about 8 ounces)

1 large yellow onion, chopped

4 ounces precooked kielbasa, sliced

½ cup dry white wine

½ teaspoon fine salt

2 teaspoons paprika

½ teaspoon cayenne

8 ounces GF radiatore or pagodas

½ cup sour cream

½ cup packed fresh parsley leaves, chopped, for garnish

Bring a large pot of salted water to a boil for the pasta.

In a large sauté pan, heat the olive oil, then add the cabbage, onion, and kielbasa. Cook over medium-high heat, stirring often, so that the onions and cabbage brown in spots as they soften, at least 5 minutes. Add the wine, salt, paprika, and cayenne and stir to mix well.

Cook the pasta. Add a few extra pieces of pasta and start checking for doneness 3 to 4 minutes before the package directs. Check often, and when it reaches al dente, drain immediately.

Add the pasta to the pan and stir, then add the sour cream and mix to coat. Scatter the parsley over it all and serve.

PISTACHIO-CILANTRO PESTO PASTA
WITH GREEN BEANS AND POTATO

Believe it or not, mixing potatoes with pasta is not a new-fangled idea. Italians have been coating pasta, potatoes, and green beans with their precious basil pesto for centuries. The new take here is the use of pistachios and cilantro, which make a creamy green sauce with a little citrusy snap.

SERVES 6 TO 8

8 ounces Yukon gold or red potatoes, cubed

8 ounces green beans, trimmed and chopped

1 cup packed fresh cilantro leaves

½ cup packed fresh parsley leaves, chopped

3 garlic cloves

½ cup shelled, raw, unsalted pistachios

1 teaspoon freshly squeezed lemon juice

½ teaspoon fine salt

6 tablespoons extra-virgin olive oil

8 ounces GF spaghetti (substitute 1 recipe Basic Fresh Pasta, page 29)

1 cup cherry tomatoes, halved

Bring a large pot of salted water to boil to blanch the veggies and cook the pasta. When the water boils, drop the potatoes in and cook for 10 minutes, then add the green beans and cook for another 5 minutes. Use a slotted spoon to scoop out the veggies to a colander. Leave the water boiling for the pasta.

While the veggies cook, make the pesto. In a food processor or blender, combine the cilantro, parsley, garlic, and pistachios and process to as smooth a purée as possible. Add the lemon and salt and scrape down, then process while drizzling the olive oil into the chute.

Cook the pasta. Add a few extra pieces of pasta and start checking for doneness 3 to 4 minutes before the package directs. Check often, and when it reaches al dente, drain immediately.

Transfer the pasta to a large bowl, add the cherry tomatoes, potatoes, green beans, and pesto and toss to mix. Serve immediately or chill for up to 2 days.

MACARONI WITH FETA, SPINACH, AND CRACKED BLACK PEPPER

Macaroni is more than just a foil for Cheddar sauce: it's a great pasta in its own right. Get a soft, melting style of feta, such as a French one, for a creamier pasta.

SERVES 4 TO 5

2 tablespoons extra-virgin olive oil

1 cup chopped red onion

2 garlic cloves, chopped

2 large red Fresno chiles (or to taste), slivered

8 ounces GF macaroni or spirals

1 teaspoon dried oregano leaves

8 ounces fresh baby spinach

½ cup pitted kalamata olives, halved

1 tablespoon freshly squeezed lemon juice

1 teaspoon freshly cracked black pepper, or to taste

4 ounces feta cheese, crumbled

Fine salt (optional)

Bring a large pot of salted water to a boil for the pasta.

In a large sauté pan, heat the olive oil and sauté the onion over medium heat. Cook for 5 to 10 minutes, until softened and browned. Add the garlic and chiles and cook until fragrant, about 2 minutes.

Cook the pasta. Add a few extra pieces of pasta and start checking for doneness 3 to 4 minutes before the package directs. Check often, and when it reaches al dente, drain immediately.

While the pasta cooks, add the oregano, spinach and olives to the onion mixture and stir until the spinach is wilted, just a couple of minutes. Add the lemon and pepper and toss. Add the pasta to the pan, then add the feta and toss until the feta melts and coats the pasta. Taste for salt: some fetas are so salty you won't need any.

Serve hot.

CABBAGE SOBA WITH CARROTS AND TRUFFLE PECORINO

It's an old Italian tradition to make a variation on fresh pasta by adding some buckwheat flour. You can use the fresh Buckwheat Pasta recipe (page 32) or our favorite Japanese noodle, 100% buckwheat soba, perfect for busy weeknights. The same nutty, earthy buckwheat flavor that makes such good pancakes is a great flavor to stand up to sweet, sautéed cabbage and truffle-scented pecorino.

SERVES 6 TO 8

2 tablespoons extra-virgin olive oil

1 medium yellow onion, chopped

3 cups slivered savoy cabbage (about 5 ounces)

2 medium carrots, julienned

2 large red jalapeños, chopped

2 garlic cloves, chopped

½ teaspoon fine salt

¼ cup dry white wine

8 ounces 100% buckwheat soba noodles or 1 recipe Buckwheat Pasta (page 32)

4 ounces truffle pecorino cheese, grated

Bring a large pot of salted water to a boil for the noodles.

In a large sauté pan, heat the olive oil over medium-high heat and add the onion, cabbage, carrots, and jalapeños. Sauté, stirring, until the cabbage is softened and browning in spots, about 5 minutes. Add the garlic, salt, and wine and continue to cook until the pan is almost dry.

Meanwhile, cook the soba according to package directions. If using fresh buckwheat pasta, cook it for 2 minutes, testing frequently. Drain and rinse with hot water, then drain again. Toss with the cabbage mixture in the pan. Toss with the cheese until it is partially melted, then serve.

BOLOGNESE SAUCE
WITH EGG CRÊPE "NOODLES"

Bolognese is a classic sauce, famous for delivering a hefty serving of savory meat. This is a protein-lovers dish, with egg crêpes and meat sauce, and hardly a carbohydrate in sight.

SERVES 4 TO 6

3 tablespoons unsalted butter

2 tablespoons minced yellow onion

2 tablespoons minced carrot

2 tablespoons minced celery

4 ounces ground pork

8 ounces ground beef

½ teaspoon fine salt

1 cup whole milk

1 cup dry white wine

1 (28-ounce) can whole tomatoes, undrained

1 recipe Egg Crêpe "Noodles" (page 38), cut into wide noodles, or 8 ounces dried GF penne

In a large, heavy pot, melt the butter over medium heat, then add the onion, carrot, and celery and sauté until the onions are translucent and soft, about 5 minutes. Add the meat and salt. Crumble the meat well as it cooks. When the meat is no longer pink, add the milk and simmer until it has evaporated, about 20 minutes, then add the wine and simmer until dry, another 20 minutes or more.

Crush the tomatoes with your hands as you add them to the pot. Add any leftover sauce from the can to the pot, then cook until the sauce is very thick.

If your crêpes are cold, warm them in the microwave or in a lightly oiled saute pan, gently turning over medium heat. Serve the egg crêpes topped with the Bolognese.

SPICY CAJUN SHRIMP PASTA

Cajun cookery is known for being spicy, but it's got lots of other flavors that back it up. This version is not too hot, and it shows off the shrimp of the Gulf Coast in a medley of fresh veggies, garlic, and a judicious amount of butter. Let the good times roll.

SERVES 4 TO 6

1 teaspoon Worcestershire sauce

1 tablespoon freshly squeezed lemon juice

1 teaspoon dried thyme

1 teaspoon hot sauce, or to taste

½ teaspoon Cajun spice blend

1 pound shrimp, peeled and deveined

2 ounces (½ stick) unsalted butter (or substitute 2 tablespoons canola oil)

2 garlic cloves, chopped

3 large scallions, chopped

1 large green bell pepper, chopped

2 cups grape tomatoes, halved

½ cup packed fresh parsley leaves, chopped

½ teaspoon fine salt

½ recipe Basic Fresh Pasta (page 29), cut into linguine, or 4 ounces dried GF linguine

Bring a large pot of salted water to a boil for the pasta.

In a medium bowl, combine the Worcestershire sauce, lemon juice, thyme, hot sauce and cajun spice and mix. Add the shrimp and toss to coat. Let marinate while you prepare the veggies.

In a large sauté pan over medium heat, melt the butter or heat the oil. Add the garlic, scallions, and green peppers and cook, stirring, until the peppers are softened, about 5 minutes. Add the tomatoes, parsley, and salt and sauté until dry. Add the shrimp and marinade and cook until the shrimp are pink and cooked through, about 4 minutes.

Cook the fresh pasta for 2 minutes, or until al dente, then drain well. If using dried pasta, add a few extra pieces of pasta and start checking for doneness 3 to 4 minutes before the package directs. Check often, and when it reaches al dente, drain immediately.

Add the pasta to the pan and toss. Season with additional hot sauce, if desired.

SOUTHERN SPICY MUSTARD GREENS AND HAM NOODLES

Spicy greens are a tradition of the American South, and they cook down to a peppery sauce to coat your pasta, much like the hearty greens enjoyed in traditional Italian pastas. A little ham goes a long way, simmering its essence into the sauce, and smoked paprika adds a hint of fire to it all.

SERVES 6 TO 8

1 tablespoon extra-virgin olive oil

4 scallions, chopped

1 medium green bell pepper, chopped

1 medium zucchini, chopped into ½-inch cubes

2 garlic cloves, chopped

1 teaspoon smoked paprika

½ teaspoon fine salt

8 ounces ham, chopped

1 (14.5-ounce) can diced tomatoes

1 bunch (12 ounces) mustard greens, washed and chopped

¾ recipe Basic Fresh Pasta (page 29), cut into linguine, or 6 ounces dried GF linguine

Hot sauce, if desired, for serving

Bring a large pot of salted water to a boil for the pasta.

In a large sauté pan, heat the olive oil over medium-high heat and add the scallions, green pepper, and zucchini. Cook, stirring, until the zucchini is browned in spots and slightly shrunken, 5 to 8 minutes. Add the garlic, smoked paprika, salt, ham, and tomatoes and bring to a boil. Stir in the mustard greens and simmer, turning the greens until they are wilted and soft, about 5 minutes. Keep cooking until the sauce is very thick, if necessary.

Cook the fresh pasta for 2 minutes, or until al dente, and drain well. For dried pasta, add a few extra pieces of pasta and start checking for doneness 3 to 4 minutes before the package directs. Check often, and when it reaches al dente, drain immediately.

Add to the greens in the pan and toss to mix. Serve with hot sauce.

QUICK JERKED PORK WITH CREAMY COLLARD NOODLES

Jerk is the Jamaican barbecue, long marinated and slowly smoked over special woods from allspice trees. We can still enjoy the flavors of jerk seasoning in this faster version, made with lean, quick-cooking pork tenderloin. Collards are similar to the callaloo greens eaten on the Island, and they make a whole meal out of this easy pasta.

SERVES 4 TO 6

1½ pounds zucchini (substitute 8 ounces GF fettuccine)

½ medium habañero chile, or to taste

3 tablespoons fresh thyme leaves

½ teaspoon ground allspice

3 tablespoons white wine vinegar

1 bunch scallions, tops and bottoms trimmed

½ teaspoon fine salt

1½ pounds pork tenderloin, thinly sliced

1 tablespoon extra-virgin olive oil

½ cup canned coconut milk, well-shaken

1 bunch (12 to 16 ounces) collard greens, thinly sliced

1 large Roma tomato, seeded and diced, for garnish

Prep the zucchini strands (pages 25 to 26) to stand in as pasta. If using fettuccine, bring a large pot of salted water to a boil.

In a blender or food processor, purée the chile, thyme, allspice, vinegar, scallions, and salt. Scrape it into a bowl and add the pork. Toss and let marinate for at least 30 minutes.

Cook the dried pasta, if using. Add a few extra pieces of pasta and start checking for doneness 3 to 4 minutes before the package directs. Check often, and when it reaches al dente, drain immediately.

To finish, heat the oil in a large sauté pan over high heat. Add the pork in batches if necessary, to avoid crowding the pan (reserve the marinade). Sear undisturbed on one side for a couple of minutes, then flip the pork pieces. Sauté until the pork is cooked and feels firm when you press it. Add the leftover marinade to the last batch of pork in the pan, and cook until the pan is dry, less than a minute. Transfer the pork to a plate and keep warm.

Add the coconut milk to the pan and stir over medium heat to deglaze all the browned spices. Add the collards and toss to coat and soften slightly, then add the zucchini or pasta and carefully toss to coat. Serve topped with the pork and garnished with the diced tomato.

WHITE SWEET POTATO NOODLES WITH COLLARDS IN SPICY AFRICAN PEANUT SAUCE

White sweet potato noodles go so perfectly with the peanut sauce—I hope that you will try them. The creamy, spicy sauce is also good with a wide, flat pasta. The strands of collard greens add to the visual impression of the pasta, but you can always try your favorite veggies in this, too.

SERVES 4 TO 6

1½ pounds white sweet potatoes or 12 ounces GF linguine

4 ounces collard greens

1 recipe Spicy African Peanut Sauce (page 48)

½ cup green sweet peas

Bring a large pot of salted water to a boil for the sweet potato noodles or the pasta.

Set up the mandoline or spiral vegetable cutter. Insert a cutter blade to make thin, ¼-inch wide slices. Trim one side of the sweet potato to make a flat surface to push against the mandoline blade; if using the spiral cutter, trim the tips and insert the potato into the machine.

Cut the sweet potato into noodle-shaped strands. Repeat with any remaining potatoes. After cutting, 1½ pounds of sweet potato should make 8 cups of strands. Roll the collard greens up around their stems, then sliver the greens. Chop the strips coarsely.

Add the sweet potato strips and collards to the boiling water. Bring to a boil again and cook for about 2 to 4 minutes. The noodles will start to break when you pick one out with a fork and will be a little firm to the bite. Drain well. If using the dried pasta, add to the boiling water. Add a few extra pieces of pasta and start checking for doneness 3 to 4 minutes before the package directs. Check often, and when it reaches al dente, drain immediately.

In the pot you cooked the potato or pasta in, heat the peanut sauce and peas, and then gently fold in the hot potato "noodles" or pasta and collards. Serve hot.

CHIPOTLE BLACK BEAN CHILI-MAC

Chili-mac is great kid food, comforting and easy to eat. This one has a little more of a grown-up air, with smoky chipotle and black beans. It's a good, fast pantry dish that you can serve up quickly, too.

SERVES 4 TO 6

1 tablespoon extra-virgin olive oil

1 medium yellow onion, chopped

2 garlic cloves, chopped

6 ounces pickled jalapeños

1 (15-ounce) can black beans, drained

1 (14.5-ounce) can diced tomatoes

1 teaspoon ground chipotle powder

1 teaspoon ground cumin

2 tablespoons sun-dried tomato paste

½ teaspoon fine salt

4 ounces GF macaroni (about 1½ cups) or penne

1 cup corn (frozen or canned)

Queso fresco (optional), for garnish

Bring a large pot of salted water to a boil for the pasta.

In a large sauté pan, heat the olive oil and add the onion. Sauté for 5 minutes, or until soft. Add the garlic and stir for a minute, then add the pickled jalapeños, black beans, diced tomatoes, chipotle, cumin, tomato paste, and salt. Bring to a boil, then reduce the heat to simmer.

Meanwhile, cook the pasta for 4 minutes less than the package directs: it will be crunchy in the center and about three-quarters of the way done. Drain the pasta and stir it into the chili mixture in the pan. Bring to a simmer and, if necessary, add a couple of tablespoons of water to loosen the chili up.

Cook for about 4 minutes, then test the pasta for doneness. When the pasta is tender and the chili is thick, stir in the corn just to heat through and serve topped with queso.

CHINESE BEEF AND BROCCOLI NOODLES

If you were missing a good stir-fry over noodles, here is the familiar beef and broccoli, made GF and with much less oil than the takeout version. Homemade Chinese food is so easy to make gluten-free, and you can use better-quality meats and veggies than your favorite hole-in-the-wall that first hooked you on beef and broccoli!

SERVES 6 TO 8

1 pound broccoli or broccolini, cut into large florets

8 ounces GF linguine or spaghetti

2 tablespoons GF oyster sauce, such as Wok Mei

1 tablespoon wheat-free tamari

2 teaspoons granulated sugar

2 tablespoons rice wine

1 teaspoon rice vinegar

¼ cup chicken stock

1 teaspoon toasted sesame oil

2 teaspoons cornstarch

1 tablespoon peanut or canola oil

1 pound steak, such as top sirloin, sliced

2 tablespoons minced fresh ginger

2 garlic cloves, minced

Bring a large pot of salted water to a boil for the broccoli and pasta. When it comes to a boil, blanch the broccoli by dropping it into the boiling water for 1 minute. Scoop out the broccoli with a slotted spoon, transfer to a colander, and rinse with cold water. Drain. Bring the water back to a boil and cook the pasta, checking for doneness 3 to 4 minutes before the package directs. Check often, and when it reaches al dente, drain immediately.

In a cup, mix the oyster sauce, tamari, sugar, rice wine, rice vinegar, chicken stock, and sesame oil, then whisk in the cornstarch.

Heat a wok or heavy skillet over high heat until hot, then add the peanut oil and swirl the pan to coat. Toss in the beef and sear briefly on one side before turning. When the outsides of the strips are browned but the insides are still pink, add the ginger and garlic and stir for a few seconds, then add the oyster sauce mixture. Stir constantly until thickened, about a minute, then add the broccoli and toss to heat through and coat with sauce. Add the noodles to the pan and toss to coat. Serve immediately.

BRAZILIAN SEAFOOD SPAGHETTI
WITH ALMONDS AND MANGO

Take your GF spaghetti on a tropical vacation with the exotic flavors of coconut milk, mango, and chopped almonds for a finishing touch. You can kick back and imagine you are on a sunny beach someplace, enjoying a ginger-spiked fish and pasta dinner.

SERVES 6 TO 8

8 ounces GF spaghetti (substitute 2 pounds spaghetti squash)

1 tablespoon canola oil

1 large yellow onion, chopped

1 large green bell pepper, chopped

1 large tomato, chopped

3 garlic cloves, chopped

1 teaspoon cayenne, or to taste

1 teaspoon paprika

1 tablespoon minced fresh ginger

1 cup canned coconut milk

1 pound firm white fish, such as cod, halibut, or perch, cubed

½ cup finely chopped almonds

1 large mango, peeled and sliced, for garnish

Bring a large pot of salted water to a boil for the pasta, or roast the squash and separate the strands (pages 25 to 26).

Cook the pasta, if using. Add a few extra pieces of pasta and start checking for doneness 3 to 4 minutes before the package directs. Check often, and when it reaches al dente, drain immediately.

In a large sauté pan, heat the oil over medium-high heat. Sauté the onion, green pepper, and tomato for about 5 minutes, then add the garlic, cayenne, paprika, and ginger. When the vegetables are almost tender, just a few minutes more, add the coconut milk, bring to a boil, and add the fish. Lower to a simmer, and when the fish is cooked through, after about 5 minutes, stir in the almonds.

Serve the fish and sauce over the spaghetti, topped with mango slices.

SRI LANKAN CURRY NOODLES
WITH CASHEWS

These spicy noodles are just as good cold as warm, so have no fear of leftovers. A quick toss in the pan and a sprinkling of crunchy cashews, and you have a great meal.

SERVES 4 TO 6

2 tablespoons canola oil

2 large yellow onions, slivered

2 tablespoons brown mustard seeds

2 garlic cloves, chopped

2 teaspoons hot curry powder

½ teaspoon turmeric

1 medium yellow squash, julienned

2 large jalapeños, seeded and chopped

2 tablespoons palm sugar or packed light brown sugar

2 tablespoons freshly squeezed lemon juice

½ teaspoon fine salt

½ cup roasted cashew pieces, coarsely chopped, for garnish

½ recipe Basic Fresh Pasta (page 29), cut into linguine, or 4 ounces dried GF linguine

Bring a large pot of salted water to a boil for the pasta.

In a large sauté pan, heat the oil over medium-high heat, then add the onions. Cook, stirring, for 10 minutes, until the onions are golden and soft. Add the mustard seeds, garlic, curry powder, and turmeric and stir for a minute, until fragrant. Add the squash and jalapeños and stir until the squash is crisp-tender, about 4 minutes. Add the sugar, lemon, and salt and stir.

Cook the pasta. Add a few extra pieces of pasta and start checking for doneness 3 to 4 minutes before the package directs. Check often, and when it reaches al dente, drain immediately.

Toss the pasta in the pan with the sautéed vegetables. Serve topped with cashews.

CHICKEN PAD THAI
WITH CILANTRO AND LIME

Pad Thai is the national dish of Thailand and a favorite of Americans who have embraced Thai restaurants with fervor. It's also really easy to make, using your GF tamari and fish sauce. In this version, you have the low-carb option of using cabbage shreds instead of noodles, which is surprisingly satisfying.

SERVES 4 TO 6

¼ cup freshly squeezed lime juice

2 tablespoons wheat-free tamari

3 tablespoons fish sauce (substitute more tamari)

2 tablespoons granulated sugar

2 large eggs

8 ounces wide rice noodles (substitute 4 cups slivered green cabbage)

¼ cup canola oil

4 garlic cloves, chopped

1 tablespoon red pepper flakes

12 ounces boneless, skinless chicken breast, thinly sliced

4 ounces bean sprouts, divided

4 scallions, cut into 2-inch pieces, divided

¼ cup dry-roasted peanuts, chopped, for garnish

½ cup packed fresh cilantro leaves, for garnish

Bring a large pot of salted water to a boil for the noodles. In a cup, stir together the lime, tamari, fish sauce, and sugar, and set aside. Crack the eggs into another cup and whisk to blend.

Cook the noodles according to the package directions. Drain and rinse with hot water.

Heat a wok or large frying pan over high heat. When hot, add the oil. Swirl to coat the pan, then add the garlic and pepper flakes, stir quickly, and then add the chicken. Sear for a minute without stirring, then stir, and keep cooking until completely cooked. If using cabbage instead of noodles, add the shreds now, and stir for 3 minutes to soften and wilt. Add the eggs, the noodles, if using, and the tamari mixture. Let the eggs set for a minute, then start stirring. When the eggs are cooked and the mixture looks more dry, about 3 to 5 minutes, stir in half of the sprouts and scallions. Scrape out onto a serving platter and top with the remaining sprouts and scallions, peanuts, and cilantro. Serve hot.

THAI MEE KROB
(CRUNCHY NOODLES WITH SHRIMP)

You knew we would have to make some fried, crispy rice noodles, didn't you? If you have never done it, rice vermicelli expands in the hot oil like a magic trick, puffing up from a handful to a panful in seconds. The texture of the airy, crunchy deep-fried noodles is addictive, and when tossed with the tangy, spicy flavors of Mee Krob, the dish becomes a festival of texture and spice. Assemble all your ingredients before starting, as the cooking goes fast and it's best eaten as soon as it's done.

SERVES 4 TO 6

PICKLED GARLIC

1 large bulb garlic, peeled and separated into cloves

½ cup rice vinegar

½ cup water

¼ cup granulated sugar

½ teaspoon salt

THAI MEE KROB

2 tablespoons granulated sugar

2 tablespoons wheat-free tamari or fish sauce

½ teaspoon tamarind paste (optional)

3 cups peanut or canola oil, or as needed for frying

4 ounces rice vermicelli

3 eggs, lightly beaten

8 ounces medium shrimp, peeled and deveined

¼ cup rice vinegar

½ teaspoon coarsely ground black pepper

1 recipe pickled garlic, sliced and drained

1 jalapeño, sliced

½ cup packed fresh cilantro leaves

1 bunch garlic chives, chopped

For the pickled garlic: combine the garlic cloves, rice vinegar, water, sugar, and salt in a small pot. Bring to a boil, then reduce the heat to a low simmer for 15 minutes. Let the garlic cool to room temperature in the liquid. Drain and chop the garlic. (You can save the liquid and use it for salad dressings; store any leftover liquid or garlic in the refrigerator.)

For the Thai Mee Krob: stir together the vinegar, sugar, tamari or fish sauce, and tamarind, if using, and set aside.

Heat the oil in a wok until very hot: it should be 375°F to 400°F. Drop a noodle in; it should float and puff up. If it sinks, the oil's not hot enough. Prepare a plate with paper towels for draining noodles as they are fried.

Fry the noodles in small batches until just puffed, a few seconds per batch. Let the oil come back up to temperature between batches. Drain the fried noodles on the paper towels.

Carefully pour out the oil into an empty can and wipe out the wok, then add 2 teaspoons of oil to the wok and place it over medium-high heat. Use a spoon to drizzle the beaten eggs back and forth across the hot wok so that they form thin strands of cooked eggs. Do not stir: they should set completely. Scoop out the eggs gently and set aside.

Stir-fry the shrimp lightly in the hot wok until pink, about 4 minutes. Add the rice vinegar and black pepper and cook until the shrimp are glazed. Add the pickled garlic, jalapeños, cilantro, and chives and toss. Serve over the fried noodles, topped with egg strands.

INDONESIAN SCALLOPS, SPINACH, AND RICE VERMICELLI

Take advantage of the speed with which noodles, scallops, and spinach cook, and you will have this tasty meal on the table in minutes. It's simply seasoned with garlic, chiles, and fish sauce—the backbone of simple rice noodle dishes from the Pacific Rim.

SERVES 4

½ cup canned coconut milk

1 large carrot, thinly sliced into coins

3 garlic cloves, chopped

1 to 2 serrano chiles, seeded and chopped, to taste

3 tablespoons fish sauce

8 ounces sea scallops, patted dry

8 ounces rice vermicelli or GF spaghetti

5 ounces fresh baby spinach, chopped

Bring a large pot of salted water to a boil for the noodles.

In a large skillet, heat the coconut milk over medium-high heat, then add the carrot, garlic, and chiles. Stir, and cook until the carrots are crisp-tender, about 2 minutes. Add the fish sauce and scallops and stir until the scallops are opaque and begin to crack around the edges, about 3 minutes.

Cook the noodles in the boiling water according to the package directions and drain. Add them to the pan, along with the spinach, tossing to mix. When the spinach is wilted, serve.

RED CURRY SCALLOPS AND SWEET POTATO WITH RICE NOODLES

Make a double batch of red curry sauce and use half of it for this. Save the rest, because you will soon be craving the addictive flavors of red curry. Scallops become meltingly tender with just a quick simmer in the deeply flavorful sauce, but you can use shrimp or cubed fish as well.

SERVES 4 TO 6

1 recipe Red Curry Sauce (page 50)

8 ounces sweet potato, cubed

12 ounces sea scallops, patted dry

4 ounces fresh baby spinach, chopped

4 ounces rice vermicelli or GF spaghetti

Bring a pot of salted water to a boil for the pasta.

Heat the curry sauce in a wide sauté pan over medium heat. When it simmers, add the sweet potato. Cook for about 10 minutes, adding water if necessary to keep it from sticking to the pan. When the sweet potato is tender when pierced with a paring knife, add the scallops and spinach and simmer, stirring, until the scallops are cooked through and the spinach is wilted, 3 to 5 minutes.

Cook the noodles according to the package directions, drain well, and pat dry with a thick kitchen towel while still hot. Toss the noodles with the scallop sauce and serve hot.

JAPANESE CURRY SOBA WITH CAULIFLOWER, TOFU, AND RED ONIONS

The idea of curry, based on the spice traditions of India, has been interpreted globally for many years. The Japanese, in particular, have made it their own and created a spiced "curry roux" that is sold in blocks and used to melt into pan sauces. Curry roux is usually full of MSG and wheat flour, so it's not safe for gluten-free diners. Fortunately, we can make a GF version and get a taste of curry from Japan.

SERVES 6 TO 8

3 tablespoons unsalted butter or canola oil, divided

3 tablespoons white rice flour

1 tablespoon Madras curry powder

½ teaspoon cayenne, or to taste

2 teaspoons Worcestershire sauce

1 tablespoon tomato paste

2 teaspoons wheat-free tamari

2 teaspoons granulated sugar

1 cup vegetable or chicken stock

1 small red onion, chopped

4 cups cauliflower florets (about half a head)

4 ounces green beans, trimmed

10 ounces firm tofu, cubed

8 ounces 100% buckwheat soba noodles

Bring a pot of salted water to a boil for the soba.

In a small saucepan off the heat, whisk 2 tablespoons of the butter or oil and the rice flour to form a paste, then whisk in the curry powder and cayenne. Place over medium heat and whisk constantly until the mixture comes to a simmer. Cook, stirring, until thickened, about 1 to 2 minutes. Remove from the heat. Whisk in the Worcestershire, tomato paste, tamari, and sugar, and gradually whisk in the stock. Place back over medium heat and whisk until the mixture thickens, about 2 minutes, then take off the heat and set aside.

Add the remaining tablespoon butter or oil to a large sauté pan and place over medium-high heat. Add the red onion, cauliflower, and green beans and stir until slightly softened, about 5 minutes. Add the tofu and gently stir. Let it brown in the pan undisturbed for a few minutes. Pour the curry sauce over the vegetables in the pan and stir, then bring to a boil. When it is boiling, reduce the heat so it simmers and cook, covered, for 4 minutes, while you cook the soba.

Cook the soba according to the package instructions and drain it, then toss it with the curry sauce and vegetables. Serve hot.

MEE GORENG (SPICY MALAYSIAN NOODLES WITH TOMATOES, AND CABBAGE)

With a confetti of colorful veggies and eggs, this quick noodle dish bears the mark of Malaysian fusion. Malays combine their tropical flavors with Chinese and other traditions to make a bowl of noodles irresistible.

SERVES 3 TO 4

1 tablespoon packed light brown sugar

2 tablespoons fish sauce

2 tablespoons wheat-free tamari

1 tablespoon Sriracha sauce

2 tablespoons Shaoxing wine or sherry

2 large eggs

½ recipe Basic Fresh Pasta (page 29), cut into spaghetti, or 4 ounces dried GF spaghetti or linguine

2 tablespoons canola oil

8 ounces boneless, skinless chicken breast, cubed

3 garlic cloves, chopped

1 cup shredded green cabbage

2 large tomatoes, chopped

2 small scallions, sliced diagonally, for garnish

Bring a large pot of salted water to a boil for the pasta.

In a small bowl, whisk together the brown sugar, fish sauce, tamari, Sriracha, and Shaoxing wine. In a separate small bowl, whisk the eggs.

Cook the fresh pasta, if using, for 2 minutes, or until al dente. Drain well. If using dried pasta, add a few extra pieces of pasta and start checking for doneness 3 to 4 minutes before the package directs. Check often, and when it reaches almost al dente, drain immediately and rinse with warm water.

Heat a large wok over high heat until very hot and smoking. Add the oil and swirl to coat. Add the chicken and stir until browned and almost cooked through, about 3 minutes. Add the eggs and stir vigorously to scramble, then quickly add the garlic, cabbage, tomato, and cooked pasta. Stir until the cabbage is wilted and tender, about 3 minutes, then pour in the sauce mixture. Keep stirring until the mixture is dry and heated through. Serve with scallions on top.

CANTONESE TOMATO–TOFU NOODLES

Invite your vegetarian friends over and serve these delicious tofu stir-fry noodles. Gluten-free hoisin and ketchup combine in a surprisingly exciting way and add instant depth of flavor.

SERVES 4 TO 6

1 tablespoon canola oil

1 small yellow onion, chopped

10 ounces extra-firm tofu, cubed

2 small tomatoes, cubed

¼ cup organic GF ketchup

2 tablespoons GF hoisin sauce

1 tablespoon wheat-free tamari

1 tablespoon chile-garlic sauce

1 tablespoon minced or grated fresh ginger

8 ounces GF spaghetti or linguine

6 large basil leaves, julienned

Bring a large pot of salted water to a boil for the pasta.

Heat a wok or large skillet over high heat for a minute, then add the oil. Stir-fry the onion for about 3 minutes to soften, then add the tofu. Stir quickly and gently, until the tofu is lightly browned, about 4 minutes. Add the tomatoes and stir until they are soft, about 2 minutes. Stir together the ketchup, hoisin, tamari, chile-garlic sauce, and ginger in a small bowl and add to the pan.

Cook the pasta to al dente according to the package instructions, checking the pasta 2 to 3 minutes earlier than the recommended cooking time. Add the pasta to the pan as soon as the sauce is hot. Stir gently to incorporate the sauce, fold in the basil, and serve hot.

KUNG PAO CHICKEN
WITH CELLOPHANE NOODLES

Make sure you turn on the hood over the stove or open a window, because burning the chiles for this dish makes the chile heat airborne, causing anyone within range to cough. It's worth it, though, because the smoky burnt chile flavor infuses the oil and the whole dish. Szechuan peppercorns make your tongue tingle, but if you can't find them, it will still be delicious without.

SERVES 4 TO 6

¼ cup rice wine or dry sherry

¼ cup wheat-free tamari

1 tablespoon granulated sugar

1 tablespoon rice vinegar

1 tablespoon toasted sesame oil

1 tablespoon cornstarch

2 tablespoons canola oil

6 whole, small dried red chiles, such as Thai

1 pound boneless, skinless chicken breast, cubed

8 ounces cellophane noodles (bean threads) or 3 (8-ounce) packages shirataki

4 ounces mushrooms, halved

1 medium carrot, julienned

1 tablespoon julienned fresh ginger

3 large garlic cloves, chopped

1 teaspoon Szechuan peppercorns, coarsely chopped

5 large scallions, cut into 1-inch pieces

1 cup toasted cashew halves

Bring a large pot of salted water to a boil for the noodles, if using.

In a small cup, mix the rice wine, tamari, sugar, vinegar, sesame oil, and cornstarch.

Preheat a wok over high heat for 2 minutes, or until it feels too hot to hold your hand an inch from the surface. Pour in the canola oil and swirl the wok to coat, then add the chiles. Cook until they start to blacken (it will happen quickly, in a minute or two), being careful not to inhale the faint smoke. Toss in the chicken and start stirring. Stir over high heat until browned but not completely cooked through, about 2 minutes.

Cook the noodles according to the package directions and drain. If using shirataki, rinse with hot water.

Add the mushrooms and carrot to the wok and stir for another 2 minutes, just until the outsides of the mushrooms look softened and slightly browned. Add the ginger, garlic, and Szechuan peppercorns, if using, and toss for a few seconds. Stir the tamari mixture and pour it into the center of the wok. Stir until the sauce has thickened, and add the scallions, cashews, and noodles or shirataki. Serve immediately.

DELHI-STYLE GREENS AND PASTA

Curry up some greens and a tangy tomato sauce, and then toss it with some nutty garbanzos and curly fusilli. A cooling dollop of yogurt adds a tangy counterpoint and a little extra protein, too.

SERVES 4 TO 6

8 ounces kale or other hearty greens

1 tablespoon canola oil

1 medium yellow onion, chopped

2 medium jalapeños, chopped, or to taste

1 tablespoon chopped fresh ginger

1 tablespoon brown mustard seeds

2 teaspoons whole cumin seeds

½ teaspoon turmeric

½ teaspoon fine salt

1 (15-ounce) can tomato purée

1 (15-ounce) can garbanzo beans drained (1½ cups)

6 ounces GF fusilli, spirals, or radiatore

1 cup plain Greek yogurt

Bring a large pot of salted water to a boil for the pasta.

Wash, stem and spin dry the kale, then chop the leaves and set aside.

Heat the oil in a large sauté pan over medium-high heat for a few seconds, then add the onions, jalapeños, and ginger. Stir until the onions are soft and sweet, about 10 minutes. Add the mustard seeds, cumin seeds, and turmeric and stir until fragrant, 2 minutes more. Add the salt and tomato purée and bring to a boil, then reduce the heat to simmer for about 5 minutes. Add the garbanzos and simmer for 5 minutes more.

Cook the pasta. Add a few extra pieces of pasta and start checking for doneness 3 to 4 minutes before the package directs. Check often, and when it reaches al dente, drain immediately.

Serve the pasta covered with the sauce and a dollop of yogurt.

COCONUT SEMIYA UPPMA

The noodles most used in Indian cuisine are very thin wheat-flour vermicelli, and they are most commonly made into desserts. This is a take on a popular quick veggie vermicelli, something that might be served for lunch or a snack.

SERVES 4 TO 6

1 tablespoon canola oil or ghee

1 teaspoon black mustard seeds

2 jalapeños, seeded and chopped

1 tablespoon chopped fresh ginger

½ teaspoon turmeric

1 large carrot, thinly sliced into coins

8 ounces green beans, cut into 1-inch pieces

1 cup corn kernels (fresh or frozen)

1 teaspoon fine salt

¼ cup unsweetened shredded dried coconut

4 ounces rice vermicelli or other thin GF noodles

Toasted cashews, chopped, for garnish (optional)

Bring a large pot of salted water to a boil for the noodles.

In a large sauté pan, heat the oil over high heat and add the mustard seeds. Stir until they start to pop. Add the jalapeño, ginger, turmeric, carrot, green beans, and corn and stir, letting the vegetables start to sizzle before reducing the heat to medium and stir-frying them to crisp-tender, about 5 minutes. Add the salt and coconut and keep stirring until the coconut is lightly golden, about 3 minutes.

Cook the noodles according to the package directions, checking a couple of minutes early just in case. Drain well, then toss with the vegetables in the sauté pan. Serve topped with cashews, if desired.

INDO-CHINESE HAKKA NOODLES WITH PANEER AND RED CABBAGE

Cultural blending is tasty on the plate, as in this delicious noodle recipe that bears the stamp of both Chinese and Indian cooks. Paneer cheese is a firm, fresh cheese that can be cubed and sautéed without melting, kind of like tofu, which is the vegan choice for this dish. If you can't find paneer, halloumi and even Cotija cheese can be used instead.

SERVES 4 TO 6

1 tablespoon canola oil

10 ounces paneer, cubed (substitute extra-firm tofu, halloumi, or Cotija cheese)

2 cups shredded red cabbage

1 large carrot, julienned

1 small red bell pepper, thinly sliced

1 cup frozen peas

2 garlic cloves, chopped

2 tablespoons wheat-free tamari

1 tablespoon rice vinegar

1 tablespoon tomato paste

1 tablespoon Sriracha sauce

1 tablespoon agave syrup or honey

1 teaspoon turmeric

1 teaspoon ground cumin

4 ounces flat rice noodles or GF linguine

Put on a pot of salted water to boil for cooking the noodles.

Heat the oil in a large sauté pan and add the paneer. Stir to coat with oil. Cook, over medium-high heat, until browned, turning every 2 minutes, for about 6 minutes.

Add the cabbage, carrot, bell pepper, peas, and garlic once the paneer is golden, and cook for about 5 minutes, or until the vegetables are tender, stirring constantly. Mix the tamari, vinegar, tomato paste, Sriracha sauce, agave or honey, turmeric, and cumin in a cup.

Cook the noodles according to the package directions, checking a couple of minutes early just in case. Drain, rinse with hot water, then drain well. When the vegetables are tender, add the noodles and the tamari mixture and stir, cooking and stirring until the sauce coats the noodles evenly. Serve hot.

RED WINE AND PARSNIP "ORZO"

Orzo pasta is small and slippery, and it easily absorbs stock, making it really flavorful. Instead of wheat-flour orzo, try this parsnip version, where pale parsnip shreds take on the flavors of red wine, sun-dried tomatoes, and stock, balancing them with the natural sweetness of root vegetables.

SERVES 4 TO 5

1½ pounds parsnips, peeled

1 tablespoon unsalted butter or olive oil

1 large yellow onion, chopped

2 ribs celery, chopped

4 sun-dried tomato halves, chopped

1 teaspoon dried thyme

1 cup red wine, such as Chianti or Merlot

¾ cup chicken stock

½ teaspoon fine salt

½ teaspoon freshly cracked black pepper

Shred the parsnips using the large holes on a box grater and set aside.

In a 4-quart pot, heat the butter or oil over medium-high heat and sauté the onion and celery for at least 10 minutes, until soft and golden. Add the parsnip shreds, sun-dried tomato halves, thyme, red wine, stock, salt, and pepper. Stir well while bringing to a simmer, and then cook uncovered, stirring frequently, for about 5 minutes. When the parsnip shreds are tender to the bite and most of the liquid is gone, serve.

AFGHAN-STYLE LAMB RICE COUSCOUS WITH PISTACHIOS AND APRICOTS

Couscous is a wheat product made from semolina wheat and is generally off-limits. Luckily, brown rice couscous is widely available and has the distinct advantage of cooking faster than brown rice. It's also got that absorbent, tender quality that you once loved about couscous, but gluten-free!

SERVES 6 TO 8

1½ pounds lamb shoulder, cut into large chunks

2 tablespoons extra-virgin olive oil

2 medium yellow onions, chopped

3 garlic cloves, chopped

1 teaspoon turmeric

1 teaspoon red pepper flakes

¼ teaspoon ground cardamom

½ teaspoon freshly grated nutmeg

½ teaspoon ground cinnamon

1 (28-ounce) can diced tomatoes

1 cup beef or chicken stock

½ cup canned coconut milk

½ cup dried apricots, chopped

2 teaspoons freshly grated lemon zest

½ teaspoon fine salt

5 ounces fresh baby spinach, coarsely chopped

1 cup brown rice couscous

¼ cup toasted pistachios, for garnish

Trim the stew meat if needed and put it on a double layer of paper towels to get the surface nice and dry. In a large pot with a lid, heat the olive oil over medium-high heat. Brown the lamb in batches, searing the outsides of the pieces before turning, then scooping them out with a slotted spoon. Put the browned lamb in a bowl and set aside. In the same pot, add the onions and sauté, lowering the heat to medium. Cook, stirring, until the onions are softened and golden, about 10 minutes. Add the garlic, turmeric, red pepper flakes, cardamom, nutmeg, and cinnamon and stir for a minute, then add the tomatoes and stock and bring to a boil. Put the lamb back in the pot with any accumulated juices and adjust the heat to a low simmer. Cook for about an hour and a half, or until the lamb is fork-tender. When the lamb is fork-tender, add the coconut milk, apricots, lemon zest, and salt, and stir. Add the spinach and cook until wilted.

Cook the couscous according to the package directions. Serve the stew over the couscous, sprinkled with pistachios.

NOTE: You can also use parsnips to make "couscous": Peel and shred 12 ounces of parsnips to make 4 cups. Prepare a steamer and steam the shreds for about 5 minutes, or until tender. Spread out a kitchen towel and transfer the parsnip shreds to the towel and pat dry (be careful because they are hot). Sprinkle lightly with salt to taste. Hold the warm parsnip shreds in a casserole dish until time to serve. Serve the lamb stew over the parsnips, sprinkled with pistachios.

BAKED PASTAS

Some of our most beloved and iconic pasta dishes are *al forno*, or from the oven. Baked pastas such as lasagna, stuffed shells, and cannelloni have the appeal of a delicious filling, a chewy pasta, a bubbling sauce, and a crusty topping, all in one rustic dish. Macaroni and cheese is good right from the stovetop, but a baked casserole melds that cheesy sauce with the noodles into the ultimate comfort food, especially when topped with crunchy, cheesy crumbs. So when the cold winds blow, you can finally indulge freely in these quintessential comfort foods.

Many of these dishes are made with dried boxed pasta to make it easier to get them on the table. The one special trick to using gluten-free pastas in the oven is this: always, always, undercook the pasta. It should be barely half-cooked—simmered just enough to make it flexible and to wash away some starches. The recipe instructions all specify this, but it is important enough to bear repeating. Your gluten-free pastas will be tender and will meld with the sauce just enough this way. If you use fully cooked pasta, it will lose texture in the oven and be less appealing.

For the adventurous, try the options using handmade crêpes or pasta sheets. Egg crêpes may seem like a project, but really, you just whisk up a simple batter, and each crêpe takes three minutes or so to cook on the stove. They can be made a day ahead and refrigerated, or even tightly wrapped and frozen, so you can have them on hand for assembling Roasted Vegetable Egg Crêpe Cannelloni with Chèvre (page 174). They also make a fine spaghetti or fettuccine substitute.

Fresh pasta is delicious in lasagna or cannelloni as well. Just make a batch of the Basic Fresh Pasta (page 29), roll it into sheets, and use what you need for the recipe. Slice what's leftover into noodles. You can even freeze them. The finished baked casseroles freeze well, too—just wrap tightly and freeze, then thaw in the refrigerator overnight before reheating in the oven.

If you were missing out on your favorite crowd-pleasing lasagnas and macaroni casseroles, they are now officially back. Yay!

SAUSAGE AND SPICY RED SAUCE LASAGNA

Dig into this deeply flavorful lasagna, studded with spicy sausage chunks, and revel in the tastes of Italy. Gluten-free lasagna noodles should be easy to find, and they work really well. This is also a good place to use fresh pasta, simply rolled out in sheets and cut to fit the pan.

SERVES 12

15 dried GF lasagna noodles or ¾ recipe Basic Fresh Pasta (page 29), rolled into sheets

1 pound fresh Italian sausage

4 cups Veggie Spaghetti Sauce (page 43)

32 ounces ricotta cheese

1½ cups Parmesan cheese, divided

2 large eggs, beaten

4 ounces mozzarella cheese, grated

Preheat the oven to 400°F. If you are using noodles that need to be pre-cooked, bring a large pot of salted water to a boil. Cook the lasagna noodles until just flexible, about 5 minutes. Drain and rinse. (If you are using fresh pasta sheets, they don't need to be parboiled.)

Lightly oil a 13 x 9-inch baking pan and line a large plate with paper towels for draining the sausage.

Heat a large skillet over medium heat. Brown the sausage for 8 to 10 minutes, or until no longer pink, crumbling it as it cooks. Transfer to the prepared plate to cool.

Meanwhile, in a medium bowl, combine the ricotta, 1 cup of the Parmesan, and the eggs. Whisk together until smooth.

Spread 1 cup of the veggie sauce over the bottom of the baking pan. Line the bottom of the pan with a single layer of pasta, trimming to fit if needed. Spread half of the ricotta mixture over the noodles, sprinkle with half of the sausage, then drizzle 1 cup of the veggie sauce over the top. Arrange another single layer of pasta on top of the sauce, pressing it lightly into the sauce. Top with the remaining ricotta mixture and sausage, then place the remaining noodles on top, pressing to make it even. Spoon the remaining 2 cups of veggie sauce over the noodles, spreading to cover. Sprinkle the mozzarella and remaining Parmesan over the sauce.

Bake uncovered for 45 minutes, or until the cheese is browned and the sauce is bubbling. Let stand 10 minutes before serving.

VEGGIE LASAGNA

If you are looking for a crowd-pleasing dish for a group that includes vegetarians, this is your home run. Everyone will love it, and the meat-free diners will get a veggie-filled, hearty main course. This veggie lasagna really lives up to its name, too, with kale, carrots, broccoli, and spinach sharing space with creamy ricotta and chèvre.

SERVES 12

2 tablespoons extra-virgin olive oil, plus more for the pan

4 garlic cloves, sliced

2 teaspoons red pepper flakes

1 (14.5-ounce) can diced tomatoes

1 (14.5-ounce) can tomato purée

1 cup canned plain tomato sauce

1 teaspoon fine salt, divided

1 bunch kale (about 8 ounces), chopped

4 ounces broccoli florets, chopped (about 2 cups)

2 medium carrots, chopped

5 ounces fresh baby spinach

15 ounces ricotta cheese

4 ounces chèvre cheese

1 large egg

15 dried GF lasagna noodles or ¾ recipe Basic Fresh Pasta (page 29), rolled into sheets

2 cups grated Asiago cheese, divided

Bring a large pot of water to boil for the veggies.

If you are using boxed noodles that need to be pre-cooked, bring another large pot of salted water to a boil and cook the pasta until just flexible, about 5 minutes. Drain and rinse. (If you are using fresh pasta sheets, they don't need to be parboiled.)

In a 2-quart pot, heat the olive oil over medium heat, then add the garlic and pepper flakes. When they sizzle, add the canned tomatoes, purée, and sauce and ½ teaspoon salt and bring to a boil. Reduce to a simmer and cook until thick, about 10 minutes.

Plunge the kale, broccoli, and carrots into the boiling water and cook for 1 minute. Then add the spinach and cook until it is wilted and dark green, about a minute more. Drain the veggies and rinse with cold water. Press against the veggies and shake the colander to extract as much water as possible. Wrap the veggies in a kitchen towel and press until very dry.

Purée the ricotta and chèvre with the egg and the remaining ½ teaspoon of salt in a food processor until smooth.

Preheat the oven to 400°F.

Lightly oil a 13 x 9-inch baking pan, then spread a few tablespoons of the tomato sauce in the pan. Line the bottom of the pan with a single layer of pasta, trimming to fit if needed. Dollop half of the ricotta mixture over the noodles, then distribute half of the veggies over that, followed by ¼ cup of the Asiago cheese. Pat down to make an even layer and drizzle with ½ cup of sauce. Repeat all the layers, then top with a final layer of noodles and the remaining sauce, spreading to cover the noodles completely. Top with the remaining Asiago cheese.

Cover the pan with foil and bake for 30 minutes. Uncover and bake for another 30 minutes, or until bubbly and golden.

VEGGIE-STUFFED JUMBO SHELLS WITH **VEGGIE-TOMATO SAUCE**

Stuffed shells are a classic comfort food, and these will deliver the comfort. They also deliver lots and lots of veggies, all cooked to melting tenderness and blended with just enough cheese to make them creamy. All that flavor and texture makes a meatless main so satisfying that you will never miss the meat.

SERVES 8

10 ounces large GF shells

Canola oil, for pan

8 ounces button mushrooms

1 medium yellow onion, coarsely chopped

1 tablespoon extra-virgin olive oil

10 ounces zucchini (about 2 small)

8 ounces kale, finely chopped

3 tablespoons fresh thyme leaves, chopped

2 garlic cloves

1 cup ricotta cheese

¾ cup grated Parmesan cheese, divided

3 cups Veggie Spaghetti Sauce (page 43)

Preheat the oven to 400°F. Bring a large pot of salted water to a boil for the pasta. Count out 36 shells and set aside. Use canola to lightly oil a 13 x 9-inch baking pan and reserve.

In a food processor, combine the mushrooms and onion and pulse to mince. Heat the olive oil over medium-high heat in a large sauté pan, and when it is hot, scrape the mushroom mixture into the pan. Change to the shredding blade in the processor and shred the zucchini. Add to the sauté pan. Cook, stirring frequently, until the mushrooms and onions are soft and the liquid is cooking off, about 5 minutes. Add the chopped kale, thyme, and garlic and keep stirring until the pan is almost dry. Transfer to a large bowl to cool.

While the filling cools, cook the shells in the boiling water for 10 minutes (or 5 minutes less than directed by the package). Drain well.

Stir the ricotta and ¼ cup of Parmesan into the mushroom mixture.

Spread 1 cup of the veggie sauce in the prepared baking pan. Stuff the shells with 2 tablespoons of ricotta filling each, then place them on the sauce, open-side up.

Spoon the remaining sauce over the shells, making sure no pasta is left bare, then sprinkle with the remaining Parmesan.

Bake uncovered for 30 minutes, or until the sauce in the pan is bubbling and the tops of the shells are golden. Serve hot.

FREE-FORM STOVETOP LASAGNA
WITH CHARD

This is in the baked pasta chapter, but this dish actually never goes in the oven. Instead, you can use fresh pasta to make individual servings of creamy ricotta-filled lasagna—all on top of the stove. The bonus is that the eggy pasta cooks to a golden brown, giving your lasagna crispy edges and a lovely chewiness.

SERVES 8

8 ounces Swiss chard, stemmed and chopped

15 ounces ricotta cheese

1 large egg

½ cup grated Parmesan cheese

1 cup packed fresh basil leaves, chopped

½ teaspoon fine salt

½ teaspoon freshly cracked black pepper

1 recipe Basic Fresh Pasta (page 29)

2 tablespoons olive oil, plus more oil for the sheet pan

2 cups Veggie Spaghetti Sauce (page 43)

RECIPE CONTINUES

Bring a large pot of water to a boil for the chard.

Drop the chard leaves into the boiling water and cook until softened and wilted, about 3 minutes. Drain and rinse with cold water. Squeeze the chard to remove all the water, then chop very finely. Wrap the chard in a kitchen towel and press to get it bone-dry.

Bring a large pot of salted water to a boil for the pasta.

In a medium bowl, combine the ricotta, chard, egg, Parmesan, basil, and salt and pepper and stir until smooth. Chill until time to use.

Cut the dough into 8 portions total. Flatten each into a rectangle and roll out in the pasta-rolling machine to 1/16-inch thick, 4 inches wide, and about 15 inches long (alternatively, you can use a rolling pin). Trim to 12-inch lengths, reserving any scraps for another use. Spread a towel on the counter and put a colander inside of a large bowl. Carefully slip two rolled-out pasta pieces into the boiling water and cook for 2 minutes, or until slightly firmer. Use tongs or a large spoon to transfer the cooked pasta to the colander to drain, then lay each piece on the towel to dry. Repeat with the remaining pasta sheets.

Lightly oil a sheet pan and place a cooked sheet of pasta on it. Scoop 1/4 cup of the ricotta filling and place it at one end of the pasta sheet to cover about one-third of the pasta. Then fold the dough back over it, press it down lightly, and put another 1/4 cup of filling on top. (Envision a piece of old-fashioned ribbon candy and you've got the idea.) Each portion should end with the remaining pasta folded over the top to cover the filling. Repeat with the remaining pasta sheets and filling.

Heat the olive oil in a large skillet over medium-high heat and when hot, use a metal spatula to carefully transfer the lasagnas to the pan. You may only be able to fit 3 or 4 without crowding: to save time, you can use 2 skillets at once. Cook for about 3 minutes, then carefully flip the lasagnas, put a lid on the pan, lower the heat to medium-low, and cook for 5 minutes more, or until the lasagnas are golden on both sides and the cheese filling is melting. Remove from the pan to individual plates.

Heat the veggie sauce separately in a small saucepan. Ladle 1/4 cup over each lasagna and serve hot.

SALMON-STUFFED SHELLS
IN LEMON CREAM

Make your pasta a little more elegant with salmon and a touch of lemon zest, all bathed in creamy sauce. This is one you will want to serve for dinner, then pack any leftovers for lunch the next day.

SERVES 8

12 ounces jumbo GF shells

1 tablespoon extra-virgin olive oil, plus more for the pan

1 large yellow onion, chopped

2 teaspoons freshly grated lemon zest

½ teaspoon fine salt

¼ cup dry white wine

1 (1-pound) salmon fillet, skinned and chopped

15 ounces ricotta cheese

1 large egg

½ cup packed fresh basil leaves, chopped

1 recipe Creamy Cheese Sauce (page 45)

Preheat the oven to 400°F. Lightly oil a 13 x 9-inch baking pan. Bring a large pot of salted water to a boil for the pasta.

Cook the shells for 5 minutes less time than the package directs: they will still have a little crunch. Drain well.

In a large skillet, heat the olive oil over medium-high heat and sauté the onion and lemon zest for about 10 minutes, or until the onions are tender and sweet. Add the salt and white wine and bring to a boil. Add the salmon and cook just until pink and almost cooked through; it will finish cooking in the oven. The wine should be mostly evaporated. Transfer the salmon mixture to a large bowl and let it cool.

When the salmon has cooled to room temperature, add the ricotta, egg, and basil and fold it all together. Use a spoon to scoop 2-tablespoon portions into each shell. Put the shells open-side up in the prepared baking pan. Spoon some of the cheese sauce over each shell so that they are all completely covered.

Bake uncovered for 30 minutes, or until the tops are lightly golden. Let cool for 5 minutes before serving.

SPINACH, BACON, AND ARTICHOKE STUFFED CRÊPE CANNELLONI

Spinach and bacon is a classic combination, and artichokes just add to the excitement. Use an extra-smoky bacon for even more bacony goodness. Eggy crêpes add flavor and protein, all while giving you that pasta texture.

SERVES 6 TO 8

Olive oil, for the pan

4 slices smoky bacon, chopped

1 medium yellow onion, chopped

14 ounces artichoke hearts (frozen or packed in water), chopped

½ teaspoon fine salt

5 ounces fresh baby spinach, chopped

1½ cups ricotta cheese

1 large egg

1 recipe Egg Crêpe "Noodles" (page 38) or ¾ recipe Basic Fresh Pasta (page 29)

2 cups Veggie Spaghetti Sauce (page 43)

1 cup shredded Parmesan cheese

Lightly oil a 13 x 9-inch baking dish. Line a plate with paper towels for the bacon.

In a large sauté pan, cook the bacon over medium heat until crisp and browned. Transfer to the paper towels to drain. Pour off all but 2 teaspoons of bacon fat. Add the onions to the pan and cook for 5 minutes, stirring. Add the artichoke hearts and salt and continue cooking for another 5 minutes, stirring occasionally. Stir in the spinach and cook until just wilted and bright green, 1 to 2 minutes. Transfer the contents to a large bowl to cool to room temperature.

When the artichoke mixture is cool, stir in the ricotta, egg, and reserved bacon.

Preheat the oven to 400°F. If using fresh pasta instead of egg crêpes, roll and cut it into ten 8 by 5-inch sheets (there's no need to par-cook them for this recipe).

Scoop ¼ cup of artichoke filling on each portion of egg crêpe or pasta and roll up, then place in the baking pan, seam-side down. Repeat until all the filling is used.

Spread the veggie sauce over the pasta rolls and sprinkle the Parmesan over the top.

Bake uncovered for 30 minutes, or until the sauce is bubbling and the cheese is melted and golden.

ROASTED VEGETABLE EGG CRÊPE CANNELLONI WITH CHÈVRE

Egg crêpes make a wonderful pasta stand-in in this delicious dish. Butter-soft roasted veggies are laced with tangy chèvre, rolled in tender crêpes, then topped with classic red sauce before being baked to crusty greatness.

SERVES 8

1 pound asparagus (tips and tender stalks only), cut into 2- to 3-inch pieces

1 pound zucchini (about 2 medium), cut into 2- to 3-inch sticks

1 medium yellow onion, thinly slivered

1 large red bell pepper, thinly sliced

1 tablespoon extra-virgin olive oil, plus more for the pan

½ teaspoon fine salt

½ teaspoon freshly cracked black pepper

3 garlic cloves, chopped

¼ cup packed fresh basil leaves, chopped

6 ounces chèvre cheese

1 recipe Egg Crêpe "Noodles" (page 38)

2 cups Veggie Spaghetti Sauce (page 43)

½ cup grated Parmesan cheese

Preheat the oven to 400°F. Combine the asparagus, zucchini, onion, and red bell pepper in a large bowl and add the olive oil, salt, pepper, and garlic. Toss to mix. Spread the veggies on 2 sheet pans and roast for 20 minutes, then stir, rotate the pans, and roast for 10 minutes more. The veggies should be tender and browning. Let the pans cool to room temperature on racks. Leave the oven on. When cool, transfer the veggies to a medium bowl and add the basil, then toss to mix.

To assemble the cannelloni, lightly oil a 13 x 9-inch baking pan. Lay the crêpes out on a counter or cutting board. Divide the chèvre and veggies among the crêpes, then roll them up and place them in the baking pan, seam-side down. Cover with the veggie sauce and then sprinkle the Parmesan down the center of the crêpes.

Bake, uncovered, for 35 to 45 minutes, or until the sauce is bubbling and the cheese is melted and golden.

MAC AND CHEESE
WITH RED CHILES AND PEAS

Everybody loves macaroni and cheese, and that's why there are three variations on the theme in this book. This Mexican-inspired one has a little kick, with chiles and lime zest adding spark to all that rich, creamy cheese. Spanish Manchego is an aged cheese with a deep, nutty flavor, and it makes this casserole a gourmet feast.

SERVES 6 TO 8

12 ounces GF macaroni or penne

1 cup fresh GF breadcrumbs or crushed GF rice square cereal

8 ounces aged Manchego cheese, grated, divided

2 ounces (½ stick) unsalted butter

2 cups 2% milk

½ cup water

2 teaspoons arrowroot starch

¼ cup white rice flour

½ teaspoon fine salt

3 small red Fresno chiles or jalapeños, chopped, or to taste

1 teaspoon freshly grated lime zest

½ cup pitted green olives, sliced

Bring a large pot of salted water to a boil for the pasta. Cook for 5 minutes less than the package directs, leaving the pasta crunchy to the bite, and drain well. It will finish cooking in the oven.

Lightly spray or butter a 2-quart glass or ceramic baking dish and set aside. Preheat the oven to 400°F.

Mix the breadcrumbs or cereal and ½ cup of the Manchego cheese in a small bowl and reserve it for topping.

Set a large sauté pan over medium heat and melt the butter. Pour the milk and water into a measuring cup and whisk in the arrowroot.

Take the pan off the heat and whisk the rice flour into the butter until it forms a very smooth paste. Return the pan to medium heat and cook, whisking, for 1 minute. Remove the pan from the heat again and gradually whisk in the milk mixture very carefully, so that you don't splash. When the mixture is smooth and all the milk is incorporated, return the pan to medium heat and whisk constantly until the milk begins to bubble. Whisk for another minute to thicken. Remove the pan from the heat and add the salt, remaining Manchego, chiles, and lime zest. Let stand for a couple of minutes to melt the cheese, then start whisking to completely melt the cheese and mix it in.

Once the sauce is melted and smooth, combine the pasta, olives, and cheese sauce in the baking dish and stir to mix. Cover with foil and bake for 25 minutes, or until the sauce bubbles around the edges. Uncover and top with the breadcrumb mixture and bake for 10 minutes more, or until the cheese topping is melted and golden.

BRAISED SQUASH, BACON, AND PENNE IN CREAM

In the depths of winter, nothing is more comforting than sweet, tender winter squash, especially baked into a creamy casserole like this. The smoky richness of the bacon and an herbal note from the fresh thyme give this dish family-friendly tastes that are sure to please.

SERVES 6 TO 8

Olive oil, for the pan

4 ounces bacon, chopped

1 small yellow onion, chopped

2 tablespoons fresh thyme leaves, chopped

2 garlic cloves, chopped

4 cups peeled and cubed winter squash (from half of a 2½-pound squash)

½ teaspoon fine salt

1 cup chicken stock

8 ounces GF penne

1¼ cups half-and-half

1 cup grated Parmesan cheese, divided

Preheat the oven to 400°F. Lightly oil a 2-quart ceramic baking dish and line a plate with paper towels for the bacon. Bring a large pot of salted water to a boil for the pasta.

Cook the penne for 5 minutes less than the package calls for: it should still be firm and a little crunchy. Drain.

Heat a large sauté pan over medium-high heat and add the bacon. Cook until the bacon sizzles and then lower the heat to medium and cook until the bacon is crisp and browned, 3 to 5 minutes, turning to cook evenly. Use a slotted spatula to transfer the bacon to the paper towel to drain.

Pour off all but 1 tablespoon of the bacon fat, then add the onions to the pan. Stir, scraping up any bits of bacon to incorporate. After the onions start to soften, about 10 minutes, add the thyme and garlic and stir. When the onions are golden, after about 5 minutes more, add the squash and stir to coat with fat. Add the salt and stock and cover the pan. Bring the stock to a boil, then reduce to a simmer over medium-low and cook for about 10 minutes. Test the squash by piercing with a paring knife.

Add the half-and-half and ½ cup of the Parmesan to the squash and stir, then stir in the pasta and coat with the sauce. Transfer it all to the baking dish and top with the reserved Parmesan.

Bake uncovered for 25 minutes, or until the cheese on top is golden and the sauce is bubbling. Cool for 5 minutes before serving.

BAKED FUSILLI, RED PEPPER, AND BROCCOLI WITH BLUE CHEESE

This pasta is a bubbling mix of green broccoli, red peppers, and fusilli, and you can add even more color if you use a mixed-veggie fusilli. We eat with our eyes first!

SERVES 6

5 tablespoons unsalted butter, divided, plus more for the pan

1 cup fresh GF breadcrumbs or crushed GF rice square cereal

4 ounces blue cheese, crumbled, divided

¼ cup white rice flour

2 cups 2% milk

½ teaspoon fine salt

¼ cup grated Parmesan cheese

8 ounces GF fusilli or spirals

4 cups broccoli florets

2 small roasted red bell peppers, peeled and chopped

Bring a large pot of salted water to a boil for the pasta. Butter a 2-quart casserole or gratin pan.

Melt 2 tablespoons of the butter and mix with the breadcrumbs or cereal and half of the blue cheese. Reserve for the topping.

In a small saucepan, melt the remaining butter over medium heat. Take the pan off the heat and whisk the rice flour into the melted butter until it forms a very smooth paste. Return to medium heat and cook, whisking, for 1 minute. Remove the pan from the heat again and gradually whisk in the milk very carefully, so that you don't spill. When the mixture is smooth and all the milk is incorporated, return the pan to medium heat and whisk constantly until the milk begins to bubble. Whisk for 1 minute to thicken. Remove the pan from the heat and add the salt, Parmesan, and remaining blue cheese. Let stand for a couple of minutes to let the cheese warm, then start whisking to melt the cheese and mix it in. Once the cheese is melted and smooth, take the pan off the heat.

Cook the pasta in the boiling water for 5 minutes less than the package directs. Drain well, then toss with the broccoli.

Transfer the pasta and broccoli to the prepared baking pan and sprinkle the chopped red peppers over the top. Pour the cheese sauce over the pasta and gently mix it in.

Cover the top with the breadcrumb mixture and bake uncovered for 25 to 30 minutes, or until the crumbs are golden and the sauce bubbles around the edges.

This dish can also be assembled up to the step of adding the crumb topping, then covered and refrigerated to bake the following day. Let come to room temperature, add the topping, and bake for 30 to 40 minutes, or until golden and bubbly.

GREEK LAMB PASTITSIO

If you love lamb, this casserole is for you. A hint of cinnamon and oregano gives the meat an exotic perfume, and you will never notice that the lamb is bulked up with minced mushrooms, making it seem even meatier. The creamy ricotta layer is a much simpler way to give it a custard topping; just purée and bake.

SERVES 8

2 tablespoons plus 2 teaspoons extra-virgin olive oil, divided

1 pound ground lamb

8 ounces mushrooms, minced in the food processor

1 medium yellow onion, chopped

1 small carrot, chopped

2 garlic cloves, chopped

1 teaspoon dried oregano

¾ teaspoon ground cinnamon

1 teaspoon fine salt, divided

1 teaspoon freshly cracked black pepper

1 (15-ounce) can tomato purée

2 cups ricotta cheese

2 cups plain Greek yogurt

2 large eggs

12 ounces GF penne or macaroni

Bring a large pot of salted water to a boil for the pasta. Preheat the oven to 400°F.

In a large pot, heat 2 tablespoons of the oil over medium-high heat and sauté the lamb, mushrooms, onion, carrot, and garlic until the lamb is cooked through, about 8 minutes. Add the oregano, cinnamon, salt, pepper, and tomato purée and simmer until thickened, about 10 minutes.

Purée the ricotta, yogurt, and eggs in a food processor until smooth.

Cook the pasta in the boiling water for 5 minutes less than the package directs. It should be flexible but still crunchy; it will cook more in the oven. Drain well and toss the pasta with the remaining 2 teaspoons olive oil and reserve.

Spread the meaty sauce in a 13 x 9-inch pan, cover with the oiled pasta, and then pour the ricotta mixture over the top and spread to cover the pasta evenly. Bake uncovered for 30 minutes. The topping will be set and browned.

GNOCCHI-VEGGIE GRATIN
WITH **AGED CHEDDAR**

Once you master the simple trick of making gnocchi, you will love serving it in different ways. In this dish, use half of your batch of gnocchi to make a Cheddary bake, with the tender cauliflower and tangy tomato singing harmony.

SERVES 6

½ recipe Potato Gnocchi (page 31) (about 2 cups)

9 ounces cauliflower, cut into florets (about 3 cups)

4 ounces aged Cheddar, shredded, divided

1 large tomato, chopped

½ teaspoon fine salt

Freshly cracked black pepper

Olive oil, for the pan

½ cup GF breadcrumbs or crushed GF rice square cereal

Preheat the oven to 400°F and oil a gratin pan or 2-quart ceramic baking dish. Bring a large pot of salted water to a boil for the gnocchi and cauliflower.

Cook the gnocchi in the boiling water in batches until they float to the surface. Remove them from the water with a slotted spoon and transfer them to a colander to drain. Reserve the boiling water.

Blanch the cauliflower in the boiling water for 2 minutes, then drain.

In a large bowl, toss the cauliflower, half the Cheddar, the tomato, and the salt and pepper with the gnocchi. Pour the gnocchi mixture into the prepared pan, then shake the pan gently to even it out. Mix the remaining Cheddar and crumbs and sprinkle over the gratin.

Bake uncovered for 25 minutes, or until the cheese on top is golden.

REUBEN PASTA CASSEROLE

If it works as a sandwich, why not make it into a pasta dish? That's the idea behind using the classic flavors of a Reuben in this intensely flavorful casserole. Pastrami, Swiss, and sauerkraut give your mouth a lively mix of tangy, spicy tastes, all baked with tender pasta for a satisfying meal.

SERVES 8

1 recipe Creamy Cheese Sauce (page 45), made with Swiss cheese

Olive oil, for the pan

10 ounces GF spirals or penne

2 cups cauliflower florets

8 ounces pastrami, chopped

1½ cups well-drained sauerkraut

8 ounces Swiss cheese, grated

Warm the cheese sauce and reserve while you prepare the rest of the ingredients. Lightly oil a 13 x 9-inch baking dish. Preheat the oven to 400°F.

Bring a large pot of salted water to a boil for the pasta and cauliflower.

Add both to the boiling water. Cook for 5 minutes less than directed on the package. The pasta should be crunchy. Drain the pasta and cauliflower well, then transfer to a large bowl. Fold in the cheese sauce and scrape the pasta into the prepared baking dish. Sprinkle the pastrami evenly over the pasta, then add the sauerkraut over that. Cover it all with Swiss cheese and pat down to make it even.

Bake uncovered for 30 minutes, or until bubbly and golden.

CREAMY SQUASH AND CASHEW CASSEROLE WITH ROSEMARY

If you are avoiding dairy, this is a veggie-rich take on a creamy baked pasta with no dairy or eggs. Raw cashews and winter squash are puréed into a creamy, cheesy-tasting sauce, making a vegan dish that is just as satisfying as one with cheese.

SERVES 4 TO 6

1 cup raw cashews, soaked in water to cover for at least 2 hours and up to overnight

2 cups water

1 cup puréed winter squash

1 tablespoon extra-virgin olive oil, plus more for the pan

1 large yellow onion, chopped

1 garlic clove, chopped

1 tablespoon fresh rosemary leaves, chopped

1 teaspoon paprika

½ cup dry white wine

1 teaspoon fine salt

8 ounces GF macaroni or penne

2 cups cauliflower florets

½ cup frozen peas, thawed

½ cup GF breadcrumbs or crushed GF rice square cereal

Preheat the oven to 400°F. Lightly oil a 2-quart glass baking dish. Bring a large pot of salted water to a boil for the pasta.

Drain the soaked cashews and put them in a blender or food processor. Grind them as finely as possible, adding the water gradually until they are a smooth purée. Add the squash and process until very smooth.

In a large sauté pan, heat the olive oil over medium-high heat and add the onion. Reduce the heat to medium and sauté until golden, at least 5 minutes. Add the garlic, rosemary, and paprika and stir until fragrant. Add the wine and salt and bring to a boil, then add the cashew mixture, whisking to combine. Bring to a simmer, then remove from the heat. It will be creamy but not really thick.

Cook the pasta in the boiling water for 5 minutes. Put the cauliflower and peas in the colander and drain the pasta over them. Add the pasta and veggies to the sauce in the sauté pan and stir to coat. Transfer to the baking dish and smooth the top. Cover with foil and bake for 30 minutes, then uncover, sprinkle with the breadcrumbs, and bake for 10 minutes more, or until the top is golden brown and it's bubbling around the edges. Serve hot.

ROASTED VEGETABLE PASTA
WITH ROASTED GARLIC SAUCE

Who says pasta needs to swim in red sauce? It's really fun—and delicious—to use other veggies as the base for pasta sauces, and this is a perfect example of the complexity and flavor that a medley of veggies can provide. Leaving part of the veggies in chunks gives it a great texture, too, and the tangy taste of yogurt and chèvre takes it over the top.

SERVES 8

1 pound eggplant, peeled and cubed

1 pound whole fennel, bulbs cubed (reserve the green tops)

8 ounces yellow squash, cubed

5 garlic cloves, peeled

2 tablespoons extra-virgin olive oil, plus more for the pan

4 ounces chèvre cheese

4 tablespoons tomato paste

½ cup plain Greek yogurt

1 cup milk

1 teaspoon fine salt

8 ounces GF penne or spirals

½ cup chopped walnuts

Preheat the oven to 400°F. Bring a large pot of salted water to a boil for the pasta. Lightly oil a 13 x 9-inch baking dish.

In a large roasting pan, toss the eggplant, fennel, squash, and garlic with 2 tablespoons olive oil. Cover the pan tightly with foil and roast for 30 minutes, shaking the pan halfway through to loosen the vegetables from the pan. At 30 minutes, uncover the pan and roast for another 30 minutes, or until the vegetables are browned and butter-soft. Leave the oven on at 400°F. Let the veggies cool slightly.

Measure out 1 cup of the roasted vegetables and pick out the roasted garlic cloves to add to the cup. Transfer the cup of veggies to the food processor and put the remaining veggies in a large bowl.

Process the veggies until puréed, then add the chèvre, tomato paste, and yogurt and process until smooth. With the machine running, add the milk and salt and process to mix well.

Cook the pasta in the boiling water for 5 minutes and drain thoroughly. Add the pasta and the puréed vegetable sauce to the large bowl with the roasted veggies. Chop enough of the reserved fennel fronds to measure ¼ cup and toss them with the pasta. Pour the pasta into the baking dish and press to even it out. Sprinkle with the walnuts.

Cover with foil and bake for 20 minutes, or until the casserole is bubbling and thick. Uncover and bake for 10 minutes more to brown the top. Let cool for 5 minutes before serving.

SPAGHETTI AND ASIAGO PIE
WITH SAUSAGE

This is a real kid-pleaser, with spaghetti, sausage, and cheese baked into an eggy wedge. It's a great one to pack in your lunch the next day, since it travels well and can be eaten at room temperature with no loss of flavor. Serve a big salad and some steamed veggies alongside, as this is mostly eggs and pasta.

SERVES 6

Olive oil, for the pan

8 ounces of your favorite pre-cooked sausage links

8 large eggs

1 tablespoon tomato paste

1 teaspoon dried thyme

½ teaspoon fine salt

2 garlic cloves, chopped

4 ounces Asiago cheese, grated

3 ounces GF spaghetti or 1 (8-ounce) package shirataki

1 large tomato, thinly sliced into rounds

Preheat the oven to 400°F. Bring a large pot of salted water to a boil for the pasta, if using. Lightly oil a deep-dish pie pan.

Chop the sausage into bite-size pieces and put in a large bowl.

In a medium bowl, whisk the eggs, tomato paste, thyme, salt, and garlic, then stir in the cheese. Cook the pasta in boiling water for 4 minutes less than the package directs, rinse, or if using shirataki, just rinse and then toss with the sausage. Transfer to the pie pan. Pour the egg mixture over the pasta and tap the surface with a spoon to level it. Place the tomato slices on top in a decorative pattern.

Bake uncovered for 30 to 35 minutes, or until the center is set and the top is browned. Serve hot or at room temperature.

CLASSIC SWEET APPLE KUGEL

This is the only sweet dish in this book, and you can serve it for lunch, dinner, or dessert. Heck, you could even have it for breakfast. Kugels are traditional Jewish dishes, but you don't have to be Jewish to love them. This sweet kugel is a creamy pudding, laced with tender noodles and studded with apples and raisins—what's not to love?

SERVES 4 TO 6

Unsalted butter, for the pan

8 ounces cottage cheese

8 ounces sour cream

¼ cup packed light brown sugar

2 large eggs

½ teaspoon ground cinnamon

4 ounces broken dried GF fettuccine or ½ recipe Basic Fresh Pasta (page 29), cut into fettuccine

1 large apple, chopped

½ cup raisins

Preheat the oven to 375°F. Bring a large pot of water to a boil for the pasta (do not salt the water). Lightly oil a 2-quart baking dish.

In a food processor, combine the cottage cheese and sour cream and process until smooth. Add the sugar, eggs, and cinnamon and process to mix.

Cook the dried noodles 3 minutes less than the package directs; they will be flexible but still crunchy. If you are using fresh pasta, cook it for 1 minute. Drain, rinse with cold water, and drain again. In a large bowl, combine the noodles, apples, and raisins and pour the cottage cheese mixture over the top. Fold it all together, then transfer to the baking dish. Bake uncovered for 45 minutes, or until the edges are puffed and the center is set. Serve warm.

SOUPS

good bowl of soup gives off waves of warm, scented steam, full of comfort and delight. Many of our most comforting soup memories involve noodles, whether you are from a chicken noodle family or a pho family. Every culture has soups with slippery, sensuous noodles or pasta floating in the bowl.

Noodle soup lovers who are gluten-free will find that adding noodles to some exciting soups is easy and fun. One thing to remember about most gluten-free pastas is that they are more fragile and more absorbent than wheat noodles. Because of that, these recipes will instruct you to add the noodles or pasta and serve immediately, or even to serve the soup over the noodles in each bowl. You can certainly eat the leftovers the next day, but you may find that your soup has gotten quite thick because the pasta soaked up all the liquids. The pasta may get softer, too, and start to dissolve.

Interestingly, Asian rice noodles and cellophane noodles seem to be very durable for a couple of days. Shirataki noodles hold up well, too. Fresh egg pasta and spaetzle are also good keepers, for a day or two.

These soups are big bowls of veggie-rich goodness, packed with flavor and fun. Two of them, Hot and Sour Egg Drop Soup (page 196) and Spicy Stracciatella with Kale (page 191), play with the idea of noodles, using eggs whisked into the simmering soup to create strands that stand in for noodles. It's a simple and direct technique—with no pasta-making skills required!—and I hope you will try it.

Take a trip with the global flavors of these soups, from the Thai Green Curry Tofu Soup with Rice Noodles (page 202) to our own Southern traditions with Catfish Gumbo with Greens and Noodles (page 207).

Make some creamy soups without flour using a few easy techniques. Corn Chowder with Smoked Salmon over Macaroni (page 206) is thickened with a purée of vegetables and made irresistible with the smoky salmon added at the end. The luscious richness of coconut milk makes several of these soups both creamy and thick, and it's dairy-free to boot.

SPICY STRACCIATELLA WITH KALE

This rustic soup is simple and easy to throw together on a weeknight, using kale and some boxed stock. The carb-phobic will appreciate that eggs take the place of noodles—they're stirred into the simmering soup and cooked into savory strands. The name *stracciatella* means "little shreds," and you will love the way the texture of the eggs pairs with hearty kale in each bite.

SERVES 4 TO 6

4 ounces kale, stemmed and chopped (about 4 cups)

6 cups chicken or vegetable stock

1 pinch red pepper flakes

3 large eggs

½ cup white rice flour

½ cup shredded Parmesan cheese

½ teaspoon fine salt

½ teaspoon freshly cracked black pepper

In a large pot, combine the kale with the stock and red pepper flakes. Bring to a boil over high heat, then reduce the heat to simmer for about 5 minutes.

While the kale simmers, whisk the eggs and rice flour together in a medium bowl, then whisk in the Parmesan, salt, and pepper. If it's lumpy, keep whisking, or process in the food processor.

When the kale looks softened and is a deep green, drizzle in the egg mixture in a thin stream while stirring the soup slowly in a circular motion (think of a whirlpool). The eggs will form strands and cook quickly, in less than 2 minutes. Serve hot.

ITALIAN SAUSAGE SOUP
WITH PASTA

A few links of sausage make this pot of beans and vegetables into a meaty stew with very little effort at all. Pick your level of spice at the meat counter. You can even use chicken sausage or vegan links for a lighter meal.

SERVES 6 TO 8

1 tablespoon extra-virgin olive oil

1 large yellow onion, chopped

3 garlic cloves, chopped

1 large carrot, chopped

1 rib celery, chopped

2 cups chopped green cabbage

12 ounces cooked Italian
  sausage, crumbled

2 tablespoons chopped fresh
  sage

1 (14.5-ounce) can diced
  tomatoes

3 cups chicken stock

½ teaspoon fine salt

8 ounces GF spirals or radiatore

Parmesan cheese, for serving

Bring a pot of salted water to a boil for the pasta.

In a large pot, heat the olive oil and add the onions. Cook over medium-high heat for about 5 minutes. Add the garlic, carrot, celery, cabbage, and sausage and stir until the vegetables start to soften, about 5 minutes. Add the sage, tomatoes, stock and salt and bring to a boil, then reduce to a simmer for about 10 minutes.

Cook the pasta in the boiling water for 4 minutes less than it says on the package, and drain it while it's still a little crunchy. Rinse and add it to the soup. Cook, stirring occasionally, for about 5 minutes, or until the pasta is completely tender.

Serve hot, with Parmesan for grating over the soup on the side.

BURMESE FISH AND COCONUT MILK SOUP WITH RICE NOODLES

A soup that is thickened with garbanzo flour is a find, especially when you can make it with GF noodles and tamari while still keeping the character of the original. This is a very noodle-filled soup, so if you want a soupier soup, cut the amount of rice noodles in half. It's a little spicy, creamy from the coconut milk, and packed with flavor—expect to be swept off your feet.

SERVES 6 TO 8

1 medium yellow onion, coarsely chopped

3 garlic cloves, peeled

1 tablespoon chopped fresh ginger

½ teaspoon turmeric

¼ teaspoon chili powder

1 tablespoon canola oil

1 to 3 large jalapeños, seeded and chopped (to taste)

2 cups chicken stock

1 (14-ounce) can coconut milk, divided

2 tablespoons fish sauce

1 teaspoon toasted sesame oil

1 small zucchini, diced

1 (8-ounce) can bamboo shoots

2 tablespoons garbanzo flour

8 ounces salmon or other meaty fish, skinned and cubed

1 tablespoon freshly squeezed lemon juice

½ teaspoon fine salt

8 ounces rice vermicelli or 6 ounces cellophane noodles (bean threads)

½ cup packed fresh cilantro leaves, for garnish

4 large scallions, slivered, for garnish

Bring a large pot of salted water to a boil for the noodles.

In a food processor or blender, purée the onions, garlic, ginger, turmeric, and chili powder.

Heat the canola oil in a large sauté pan over medium-high heat and fry the purée with the jalapeños.

When the mixture is golden brown and beginning to stick to the pan, in about 4 minutes, add the stock, ½ cup of the coconut milk, and the fish sauce, sesame oil, zucchini, and bamboo shoots. In a large measuring cup, whisk the remaining coconut milk with the garbanzo flour and stir it into the pot. Bring to a boil, stirring, and then reduce to a simmer for 5 minutes.

Add the fish and bring back to a simmer, just until the fish is cooked, 3 to 4 minutes. Stir in the lemon and salt and remove from the heat.

Cook the noodles according to the package instructions and then drain. Serve the noodles with soup ladled over them and garnished with cilantro and scallions on top.

LAKSA LEMAK

Laksa is a dish served in Malaysia and Singapore, and it brims with the flavors of lemongrass, tamarind, and ginger. Vegetarians can skip the shrimp and add tofu. Enjoy it with rice noodles, GF linguine, or shirataki.

SERVES 6 TO 8

1 tablespoon canola oil

1 large yellow onion, chopped

3 garlic cloves, chopped

1 stalk lemongrass, split and cut into 4-inch pieces

1 (14-ounce) can coconut milk

3 cups vegetable or chicken stock

1 tablespoon tamarind paste

1 teaspoon red pepper flakes

1 teaspoon ground coriander

½ teaspoon turmeric

1 tablespoon chopped fresh ginger

3 tablespoons fish sauce

1 tablespoon granulated sugar

1 large red bell pepper, sliced

4 ounces Cellophane noodles (bean threads)

1 pound shrimp, peeled and deveined

½ cup slivered basil or mint, for garnish

Bring a large pot of salted water to a boil for the noodles.

In a large pot, heat the canola oil over medium-high heat. Add the onion, garlic, and lemongrass and sauté until the onion is soft and translucent, about 5 minutes. Add the coconut milk, stock, tamarind, red pepper flakes, coriander, turmeric, ginger, fish sauce, and sugar. Bring to a boil, then reduce to a simmer and cook for 10 minutes. Add the bell peppers and cook for 5 minutes, or until they have softened.

Cook the noodles in the boiling water according to the package directions, then drain.

Add the shrimp to the coconut milk mixture and continue simmering until the shrimp are pink and cooked through, 3 to 4 minutes. Stir in the noodles. Serve hot, garnished with basil or mint.

HOT AND SOUR EGG DROP SOUP

Like the stracciatella, egg drop soup is a Chinese example of the ease with which eggs form noodle-like streamers in a simmering broth. Most egg drop soup is pretty plain, so I jazzed it up with hot and sour zing, which has the side benefit of the vinegar making the eggs a little firmer.

SERVES 4 TO 6

4 cups vegetable or chicken stock

1½ tablespoons cornstarch

2 teaspoons freshly cracked black pepper

¼ cup rice vinegar

2 tablespoons wheat-free tamari

1 teaspoon sesame oil

4 large eggs, whisked (substitute 2 cups slivered cabbage)

1 large carrot, finely julienned

4 ounces sugar snap peas (about 1½ cups), trimmed

Pinch of salt (optional)

5 medium scallions, sliced diagonally

Heat the stock in a large pot over medium heat. Combine the cornstarch and pepper in a small bowl. Whisk the vinegar, tamari, and sesame oil into the cornstarch mixture. Whisk the eggs in a 2-cup measuring cup with a pouring spout or in a medium bowl.

Pour the cornstarch mixture into the hot stock, whisking to blend. Bring the mixture to a boil. Stir the carrots and peas (and cabbage, if using) into the stock and simmer for about 3 minutes. Taste the soup: depending on the saltiness of your stock, you may want to add a pinch of salt. Stir the scallions into the soup. Stir the soup slowly in a circular motion as you drizzle in the eggs in a steady stream, making strands of cooked egg (think of a whirlpool here). Remove from the heat as soon as the eggs are cooked, about 2 minutes, and serve right away.

FAST PHO

Pho is a beloved street food in Vietnam, where vendors carry steaming canteens of broth to pour over fresh ingredients in the bowl as each customer orders. The hot broth poaches the thinly sliced ingredients just enough, and heaps of fresh herbs and chopped chiles give it a light, fresh quality. Pho is usually all about the time-consuming broth, but we can cut a step and use boxed stock to delicious results.

SERVES 6 TO 8

2 teaspoons canola oil

3 slices fresh ginger

4 garlic cloves, thinly sliced

8 cups chicken stock

2 whole star anise

1 stick cinnamon

1 teaspoon black peppercorns

3 tablespoons fish sauce or wheat-free tamari, or more to taste

4 small baby bok choy, cut into 2-inch pieces

16 large shrimp, shelled and deveined

1 large carrot, julienned

8 ounces fried tofu, sliced

2 to 3 jalapenos, seeded and chopped (or to taste, optional)

2 cups bean sprouts

3 ounces flat rice noodles or GF fettuccine

4 large scallions, sliced diagonally

2 large limes, halved and sliced

Sriracha, for serving (optional)

Bring a large pot of salted water to a boil for the noodles.

In a 2-quart pot, heat the oil over medium-high heat, then sauté the ginger and garlic just until fragrant, about a minute. Add the stock, anise, cinnamon, peppercorns, and fish sauce or tamari. Bring to a simmer and then reduce the heat to keep it at a gentle bubble. Cook for 20 minutes, uncovered. The stock will reduce to about 7 cups.

While the stock takes on flavor, prepare the garnishes. Place the bok choy, shrimp, carrot, tofu, jalapenos, if using, and bean sprouts in separate piles on a plate or two.

Cook the noodles according to the package directions, drain and rinse with warm water, and divide them between 6 to 8 wide soup bowls.

When the stock is ready, strain it through a fine-mesh sieve, taste for salt, adding more fish sauce or tamari if you think it needs it, and bring it to a boil over high heat when ready to serve. To serve, the traditional method is to put the shrimp, tofu, and vegetables on top of the noodles and ladle boiling stock over them to cook them lightly. Serve with scallions piled on top and lime wedges and Sriracha on the side. If desired, you can lightly cook the shrimp, bok choy, and carrot in the simmering stock and serve the soup from a communal pot, ladling it over the rice noodles and tofu in each bowl and garnishing with scallions.

SOPA SECA WITH GARBANZOS

Sopa Seca, or "dry soup," is a traditional Mexican way to enjoy noodles. Usually, thin wheat vermicelli are fried and then tossed in a soup to absorb broth and cook that way. Here, we skip the pesky frying and blanch the noodles just to start the hydrating process, then finish in the tasty broth.

SERVES 4 TO 6

1 tablespoon canola oil

4 garlic cloves, sliced

1 cup diced zucchini

2 ears corn on the cob, kernels removed

1 (15-ounce) can fire-roasted tomato purée

½ teaspoon ground chipotle pepper

1½ cups cooked garbanzo beans, drained

1 teaspoon dried oregano

½ teaspoon freshly ground black pepper

½ teaspoon fine salt

1 cup vegetable stock, plus more as needed

8 ounces GF spaghetti or rice noodles, broken into 1-inch pieces

4 ounces queso fresco, crumbled, for garnish

Fresh cilantro leaves, for garnish

Bring a pot of salted water to a boil for the pasta.

In a large pot, heat the canola oil over medium-high heat and sauté the garlic until fragrant and lightly golden, about a minute. Add the zucchini and corn and sauté until golden, about 5 minutes. Add the tomato purée, ground chipotle, garbanzos, oregano, black pepper, and salt and stir to mix well, then add stock and bring to a boil. Reduce heat to a simmer, stirring, until the veggies are al dente, adding more stock if needed, about 3 minutes.

Cook the pasta in the boiling water for 3 minutes less than directed on the package: it will be flexible but crunchy. Drain and rinse with hot water, then add to the simmering soup and stir until the noodles are fully tender, about 5 minutes. They will absorb the liquids, and you may need to stir in a tablespoon or two of stock to keep the noodles from sticking to the pan Test the noodles by taking a bite. When tender, take off the heat and serve, topped with queso and cilantro.

KIMCHI NOODLE SOUP WITH CHICKEN

Kimchi is a magical shortcut ingredient, full of tangy fermented flavors and spice. Adding it to this easy chicken soup gives it a Korean flavor and adds healthy cabbage with very little effort. Your noodles will swim in a rich, miso-scented broth, warming you from the inside out.

SERVES 6 TO 8

1 pound boneless, skinless chicken thighs

4 cups chicken stock

1 medium yellow onion, chopped

1 medium carrot, sliced diagonally

2 garlic cloves, chopped

2 tablespoons dark miso

1 tablespoon sesame oil

1 tablespoon wheat-free tamari

2 cups kimchi, chopped

2 teaspoons Sriracha sauce (optional)

1 pound shirataki or 8 ounces 100% buckwheat soba noodles

4 medium scallions, slivered, for garnish

If using soba noodles, bring a large pot of salted water to a boil for the noodles.

Chop the chicken into bite-size pieces and reserve. In a large pot, over high heat, heat the chicken stock and add the onions and carrots. When it comes to a boil, reduce to a simmer. Cook for about 5 minutes to soften the vegetables. Add the garlic and chicken and simmer for another 5 minutes. In a cup, stir together the miso, sesame oil, and tamari, then stir it into the soup. Stir in the kimchi and simmer gently for about 5 minutes. Taste the soup for heat: if you want it hotter, add the Sriracha sauce.

Cook the soba noodles, if using, and start checking for doneness 2 minutes before the package directs. Drain and rinse with hot water. If using shirataki noodles, simply rinse and drain.

You can add the noodles to the soup either by stirring them in or by portioning them into bowls and ladling the soup over them. Sprinkle with scallions and serve.

SPAETZLE CHICKEN SOUP
WITH CARROTS

Show off your handmade spaetzle in this really simple soup, which you can assemble and have simmering while you make the spaetzle. It's a little bit German, so serve it with your fave wurst and a gluten-free beer.

SERVES 6 TO 8

1 tablespoon extra-virgin olive oil

1 medium yellow onion, chopped

2 ribs celery, chopped

1 medium carrot, chopped

12 ounces cubed chicken breast

4 cups chicken stock

1 bay leaf

1 teaspoon dried thyme

½ teaspoon freshly cracked black pepper

½ teaspoon fine salt

1 recipe Easy Spaetzle (page 30)

2 cups packed fresh baby spinach, chopped

For the soup, heat the olive oil in a large pot over medium-high heat. Add the onions, celery, and carrot, and stir. Cook for about 10 minutes, or until softened. Push the veggies to one side of the pot and add the chicken. Stir and sauté until browned, about 5 minutes. Add the stock, bay leaf, thyme, pepper, and salt, and bring to a boil, then reduce to a low simmer. Simmer for about 10 minutes to cook the chicken and carrots through. Remove the bay leaf.

Add the cooked spaetzle to the soup with the chopped spinach and stir until the spinach wilts and the spaetzle is warmed through. Serve hot.

THAI GREEN CURRY TOFU SOUP
WITH RICE NOODLES

Missing that soup you used to get at the Thai place because they just can't get with your gluten-free program? All the flavors are here, with an abbreviated version of homemade curry paste that comes together in your food processor or spice grinder instead of coming out of a jar. If you are not a fan of spicy heat, use fewer chiles in the curry paste. Cellophane noodles are a good choice here, and the clear noodles glisten in the spicy curry.

SERVES 6 TO 8

1 small stalk lemongrass, trimmed and sliced

1 to 3 medium serrano chiles, seeded, to taste

2 large shallots, peeled

1 inch fresh ginger, peeled

4 garlic cloves, peeled

1 teaspoon ground coriander

1 teaspoon ground cumin

¼ cup minced cilantro stems

1 teaspoon canola oil

1 (14-ounce) can coconut milk

1 cup chicken or vegetable stock

1 tablespoon packed light brown sugar

¼ cup fish sauce or wheat-free tamari, or more to taste

14 ounces firm tofu, drained

2 large carrots, chopped

1 cup frozen peas, thawed

1 tablespoon freshly squeezed lime juice

4 ounces Cellophane noodles (bean threads) or ½ recipe Basic Fresh Pasta (page 29), cut into spaghetti

1 cup packed fresh Thai basil leaves, slivered, for garnish

Bring a large pot of salted water to a boil for the noodles.

First, make the curry paste. In a spice grinder or food processor, combine the lemongrass, serranos, shallots, ginger, garlic, coriander, cumin, and cilantro stems. Process to grind as finely as possible.

In a large pot, heat the canola oil over medium heat and add the paste. Cook, stirring and scraping, until the paste darkens and thickens, about 3 minutes.

Add the coconut milk, stock, brown sugar, and fish sauce or tamari and bring to a boil. Lower the heat to a simmer and add the tofu and carrots. Cook until the carrots are crisp-tender, about 3 minutes. Stir in the peas and lime juice and taste, adding more fish sauce or tamari if needed.

Cook the noodles noodles in the boiling water according to the package directions. If using fresh pasta, cook it for 2 minutes, or until al dente. Drain well and add the noodles to the hot soup. Serve topped with fresh basil.

CAJUN CRAB, GREENS, AND NOODLE SOUP

Down South, crabs are a local delicacy. This soup captures the spirited spice of Cajun cuisine and is a delicious way to make a small amount of crab go a long way. If you feel like splurging, buy king crab legs, thaw them, and use kitchen shears to cut the shells open so you can extract large chunks of the tender white flesh. Then simply tear it into bite-size chunks and drop it in the soup. If you opt for canned, look for the cans in the cold case, called pasteurized crab, and search on the label for "lump," which means there are bigger pieces. I like this with sweet potato strands, but you can use broken linguine, shells, or macaroni, too.

SERVES 6 TO 8

¼ cup canola oil or extra-virgin olive oil

6 tablespoons white rice flour

1 tablespoon Cajun seasoning

2 garlic cloves, chopped

3 (8-ounce) bottles clam juice

1 (14.5-ounce) can diced tomatoes

1 (15-ounce) can tomato purée

2 tablespoons fresh thyme leaves, chopped

8 ounces collard greens, stemmed and chopped

8 ounces white sweet potato, spiral cut into strands (about 2 cups) (page 25 to 26)

12 ounces crabmeat (from about 24 ounces whole king crab legs, or use pasteurized canned meat)

Bring a large pot of salted water to a boil for the sweet potato.

In a large pot off the heat, whisk together the oil and rice flour until smooth. Place over medium heat, whisking until it starts to bubble. Cook for a couple of minutes, then add the Cajun seasoning and garlic, and reduce the heat to low. When thick and browned, about 5 minutes, slowly pour in the clam juice, then add the diced tomatoes, tomato purée, thyme, and greens. Bring to a boil, then reduce the heat to a simmer and cook until the greens are soft, 5 minutes.

Blanch the sweet potato noodles in the boiling water for 2 minutes. Drain well. Stir the crabmeat and noodles into the soup just before serving. Heat through and serve.

MEXICAN SWEET CORN AND PEPPER SOUP WITH SHRIMP

If you crave Mexican food but think it only consists of tacos and burritos, break out with this light, colorful soup. It's simple and easy to prepare, and it celebrates the veggies and fresh seafood of Mexico. Noodles make it more stick-to-your-ribs filling, and kids will love it, too.

SERVES 4 TO 6

1 tablespoon extra-virgin olive oil

1 large yellow onion, chopped

1 garlic clove, chopped

1 medium red bell pepper, chopped

2 large jalapeños, chopped

1 teaspoon ground cumin

1 tablespoon fresh thyme leaves, chopped

4 cups chicken or vegetable stock

½ teaspoon fine salt, or more to taste

1 cup corn (fresh or frozen)

1 small zucchini, diced

1 pound shrimp, peeled and deveined

4 ounces GF spaghetti (substitute 2 cups of any noodles)

1 large lime, halved

1 avocado, diced

Fresh cilantro leaves, for garnish

Queso fresco, for garnish (optional)

Bring a large pot of salted water to a boil for the pasta.

In a large pot, heat the olive oil over medium-high heat. Add the onion, garlic, red bell pepper, and jalapeño and sauté for 5 minutes. Add the cumin and thyme and sauté for another 5 minutes, or until fragrant. Add the stock, salt, corn, and zucchini and bring to a boil, then reduce to a simmer. Cook for 10 minutes, or until the zucchini is crisp-tender. Add the shrimp and simmer just until they turn pink. Taste for salt and add more if necessary.

Cook the pasta in the boiling water until al dente, checking for doneness 3 minutes before the package directs. Drain the pasta and stir it into the soup. Squeeze a little lime juice over the avocado, then cut the lime halves into wedges. Serve bowls of soup with lime-doused avocado cubes and lime wedges on the side. Sprinkle with cilantro and queso, if desired.

BAHAMIAN CHOWDER WITH COD

Take a cruise and visit the islands, where fish is as fresh as it can be. In this creamy coconut chowder, a ripe plantain provides a fun change from the usual vegetables. If you are unfamiliar with plantains, they look like big bananas but are starchy and not sweet. For this soup, let the plantain ripen until the skin is black, then use a knife to pare away the skin.

SERVES 6 TO 8

1 tablespoon unsalted butter

1 medium carrot, chopped

1 large bay leaf

1 medium yellow onion, sliced

1 small red bell pepper, chopped

1 small green bell pepper, chopped

1 ripe plantain, sliced

1 (14-ounce) can coconut milk

1 (15-ounce) can whole tomatoes, undrained

½ teaspoon fine salt

½ cup packed fresh parsley leaves, chopped

1 tablespoon Jamaican curry powder

¼ teaspoon cayenne

1 pound cod, cubed

6 ounces GF spaghetti

Bring a large pot of salted water to a boil for the pasta.

In a large pot, melt the butter over medium heat. Add the carrot, bay leaf, onion and red and green peppers and stir. Cook, stirring often, for about 10 minutes. The peppers should be softened and the onion golden. Add the plantain and stir for a minute, then add the coconut milk, tomatoes (crushing with your hands as you go), salt, parsley, curry powder, and cayenne. Increase the heat to medium-high and bring to a boil, then reduce the heat and simmer for 5 minutes to blend the flavors and cook the plantain through. The plantain should have the texture of a cooked potato when pierced with a knife. Add the cod and simmer just until the fish is cooked, about 5 minutes more.

Cook the pasta until almost al dente, leaving it a teeny bit crunchy, about 4 minutes less than the package directs. Drain and stir the pasta into the soup and cook gently until the pasta is tender, a few minutes more. Serve hot.

CORN CHOWDER WITH SMOKED SALMON OVER MACARONI

Sweet, creamy corn chowder studded with smoky salmon is a hit, especially because the veggie purée does all the thickening: no flour required. I enjoy this one over macaroni, like a classy version of chili mac. Vegetarians can use smoked tempeh or tofu in place of the fish.

SERVES 4 TO 6

2 teaspoons olive oil

1 medium yellow onion, chopped

2 (10-ounce) bags frozen corn, thawed

½ medium red bell pepper, diced

1½ cups milk, plus more as needed

½ teaspoon fine salt

1 pinch freshly cracked black pepper

4 dashes hot sauce, or to taste

2 tablespoons minced parsley, plus 4 to 6 sprigs for garnish

4 ounces hot-smoked salmon, broken into chunks

8 ounces GF macaroni or small shells

Bring a large pot of salted water to a boil for the pasta.

In a large pot, heat the olive oil over medium-high heat. Sauté the onions until golden, about 10 minutes. Add the corn, red bell pepper, and milk and bring to a boil, then reduce the heat to barely simmer. Cook for about 5 minutes, or until the red bell pepper is softened.

Scoop half of the corn mixture into a food processor or blender and carefully purée until smooth. Scrape it back into the pot. Heat the mixture over medium heat, stirring, just until hot. If desired, stir in more milk to make a thinner soup. Add the salt, black pepper, hot sauce, and minced parsley and stir in the salmon chunks.

Cook the pasta according to the package directions, then drain. Serve the macaroni in bowls, topped with a ladle of corn chowder and a sprig of parsley.

CATFISH GUMBO
WITH GREENS AND NOODLES

Gumbo has two things Northerners may not be accustomed to eating: okra and filé powder. Okra, when fresh, has a nice crispness and a unique, sweet flavor, and it also gives off a natural thickener that binds the soup a bit. You can use frozen, too, although that will be very soft. Filé powder is ground sassafras leaves, and it also thickens the soup. It is a classic flavor, beloved of Southerners. You can serve the filé at the table to sprinkle in to taste if it is new to you.

SERVES 4 TO 6

2 tablespoons canola oil or unsalted butter

1 medium yellow onion, chopped

1 rib celery, chopped

1 green bell pepper, chopped

2 scallions, chopped

3 garlic cloves, chopped

2 tablespoons white rice flour

½ teaspoon hot sauce

1 (14.5-ounce) can diced tomatoes

6 cups chicken stock

1 cup trimmed and sliced okra

1 teaspoon dried thyme

1 teaspoon dried oregano

4 ounces cooked andouille sausage, sliced

½ bunch mustard greens or other hearty greens, chopped (about 6 ounces)

½ teaspoon fine salt

½ teaspoon freshly cracked black pepper

2 teaspoons filé powder, or to taste (optional)

4 ounces GF spaghetti or linguine, broken into 2-inch pieces

8 ounces catfish, tilapia, or cod, cut into chunks

Bring a large pot of salted water to a boil for the pasta.

In a large pot, heat the oil or butter over medium heat and add the onion, celery, bell pepper, scallions, and garlic and sauté for 5 minutes. Add the flour and cook 2 minutes more, then add the hot sauce and tomatoes and simmer for a minute. Add the stock, okra, thyme, oregano, andouille, and mustard greens. Bring to a boil, then reduce the heat and simmer for 30 minutes. Add the salt and pepper and filé, if desired, and stir.

Cook the pasta in the boiling water, checking for doneness 3 to 4 minutes before the package directs. Check often, and when it reaches al dente, drain immediately.

Add the fish to the pot and simmer to cook through, about 5 minutes. Serve the pasta in bowls and cover with the gumbo.

INDIAN SPINACH SOUP WITH CHILES AND VERMICELLI

It's common to see dals and curries with beans, but not so common to have one with mostly veggies. This delicious soup is very green, with lots of tender spinach, and is thickened with a potato instead of flour. Thin vermicelli is perfect here, and a dollop of raita on top makes the meal complete.

SERVES 4 TO 6

1 tablespoon unsalted butter or canola oil

1 medium Yukon gold potato, thinly sliced

2 tablespoons chopped fresh ginger

2 garlic cloves, chopped

2 medium jalapeños, chopped, or to taste

1 teaspoon ground coriander

½ teaspoon turmeric

4 cups vegetable stock

10 ounces fresh baby spinach

¾ cup tomato purée

4 ounces rice vermicelli (substitute 8 ounces shirataki)

1 cup fat-free plain Greek yogurt

½ cup diced cucumber

1 teaspoon ground cumin

½ teaspoon fine salt, or more to taste

Bring a large pot of salted water to a boil for the noodles.

Melt the butter or canola oil in a large pot over medium heat, then add the potato, ginger, garlic, jalapeños, coriander, and turmeric. Sauté until the spices are fragrant, 1 to 2 minutes. Add the stock, cover, and bring to a boil. Reduce heat and simmer, covered, for 15 minutes. Uncover and check the potatoes; they should be soft. Stir in the spinach and simmer until it is soft and bright green, about 3 minutes. Stir in the tomato purée.

Carefully transfer the contents of the pan to a blender. Using a folded kitchen towel, hold the lid on tightly so the hot soup stays safely inside the blender as you purée. Process until very smooth. Pour back into the pot and keep warm.

Cook the noodles according to the package directions until just al dente. Drain, rinse, and add to the soup. (If using shirataki, just rinse and add to the soup.) Stir and heat through.

For the raita, stir together the yogurt, cucumber, cumin, and salt. Ladle the soup into bowls, swirl about 3 tablespoons of raita into each, and serve.

INDEX

Note: Page references in *italics* indicate photographs.